Arthur, Louise and the True Hound of the Baskervilles

Arthur, Louise and the True Hound of the Baskervilles

by

Margaret Newman Turner

Logaston Press

LOGASTON PRESS
Little Logaston Woonton Almeley
Herefordshire HR3 6QH
www.logastonpress.co.uk

First published by Logaston Press 2010
Copyright © Margaret Newman Turner 2010

ISBN 978 1906663 36 0

Typeset in Baskerville by Logaston Press
and printed in Great Britain by
Bell & Bain Ltd, Glasgow

Front cover photograph of Hergest Court © John Mason

For my Father

*Statue of Arthur Conan Doyle in Crowborough
by the sculptor David Cornell (Brian W. Pugh)*

Contents

Works consulted

Arthur Conan Doyle, *Angels of Darkness*, ed. Peter Blau, The Baker Street Irregulars, New York, 2001

Arthur Conan Doyle, *Sherlock Holmes: the Complete Short Stories*

Arthur Conan Doyle, *The Stark Munro Letters*, 1895

'Celebrities at Home: a Day with Conan Doyle', article for the *Strand Magazine*, August 1892

Andrew Lycett, *Conan Doyle: The Man Who Created Sherlock Holmes*, Weidenfeld and Nicolson, 2007

Dr. Andrew Norman, *Arthur Conan Doyle: Beyond Sherlock Holmes*, NPI Media Group, 2007

Jon Lellenberg, Daniel Stashower & Charles Foley, *Arthur Conan Doyle: A Life in Letters*, HarperPress, 2007

Acknowledgements

There are many people to whom I am indebted, but my special thanks go to: Peter Blau, Secretary of 'The Baker Street Irregulars', USA; Ian Cooke; Mrs. Georgina Doyle, widow of Brigadier John Doyle; Mrs. Anne Edwards for deciphering my longhand; Professor Christopher Frayling, Rector and Vice Provost of the Royal College of Art; Mrs. Anne Goodwin; Mrs. Margaret Hawkins; Mrs. Gillian Hodges; Mr. Bob Jenkins; Mrs. Margaret Picknill; and Mr. Brian Pugh, Curator of the Conan Doyle (Crowborough) Establishment. My thanks also to the staff of Brecon Military Museum; Powys Archives; Gloucester Archives; Hereford Reference Library; Hereford Museum; Presteigne Library; and the Judges Lodging Museum, Presteigne; and to Andy and Karen Johnson of Logaston Press, who also contributed with artistic design. Also I must thank all my friends, who encouraged me and listened with patience to my ideas!

Whilst I have endeavoured to check all the details included in this book, any errors and inaccuracies remain my responsibility.

Margaret Newman Turner
Presteigne
April 2010

Introduction

A letter to my father written and signed by Arthur Conan Doyle was sold by Bonhams in London on 18 March 2008, and aroused so much interest that I felt the time had come to research it in more detail. My strong conviction, and that of many others, is that the book *The Hound of the Baskervilles* was based on the legend of the Hound of the Vaughans of Hergest, and that Conan Doyle was told this legend by his first wife Louise (née Hawkins), whose family had lived and farmed in the Welsh Border country for hundreds of years.

I begin by telling the Legend as it was told to me by my father. A solicitor by profession, he was born and bred only two miles from Hergest Court, and his ancestors also go back a long way around the Welsh Border. That is followed by an account of Arthur Conan Doyle's life, and especially his marriage to Louise. It has now been realised that this period of his life has been largely ignored. Sherlockians are well aware that the invention and writing of the first two dozen or so Sherlock Holmes stories, now known as the *Adventures* and the *Memoirs of Sherlock Holmes*, which formed the basis of Conan Doyle's fame and fortune, were written in the first few years of his first marriage. (Few people now remember his historical novels or his other short stories, except perhaps *The Lost World*.) Louise, called 'Touie' by Arthur Conan Doyle, was *always* by his side during this time. She was his love, his inspiration and his muse. She almost certainly told Arthur of the story of the Black Hound of Hergest, and may have encouraged him to read *Malvern Chase* by W.S. Symonds, which uses the story of the hound.

Georgina Doyle's book *Out of the Shadows*, published in 2004, is the only account I have read to show the true feelings of the Doyle family about Arthur's second marriage. I was not able to read it until last year (2009), but I have now met Georgina. I asked her if she would mind my publishing this book, and making Louise Hawkins my chief subject, and she said indeed no, it would back up her own findings.

I have added a little about the Baskerville family. Ralph Baskerville, who gave his life on the Western Front in 1918, was a fine character, and my father knew him (there were only three years between them).

I have also included some interesting statements from people who have seen the Hound of the Vaughans, one by my grandmother, and the correspondence between Conan Doyle and my father. And finally, the BBC having put on a dramatic production of the 'Hound of Hergest' in 1934, I enclose the correspondence between my father, the scriptwriter, Miss Enoch, and the producer, the famous Martin Webster, who was with the BBC for many years.

Appendix 4 says a little about Hergest Court and the surrounding area.

Chapter 1
The Hound of the Vaughans

Holmes leaned forward in his excitement, and his eyes had the hard,
dry glitter which shot from them when he was keenly interested.
　　　'You saw this?'
　　　'As clearly as I see you.'
　　　'And you said nothing?'
　　　'What was the use?'

The Hound of the Baskervilles

The legend of the Hound of the Vaughans has been of great interest to me from childhood. My father took me to Hergest Court, and I saw the haunted room and the lake, and gazed at Castle Twts. My father was a solicitor with his own practice at 7 Grosvenor Gardens in London, and we lived at Limpsfield in Surrey. Born in 1878, he was the son of Philip Turner of Arrow Lodge Mills, Kington (the 'P.' standing for 'Philip' is part of the firm's name, 'J. & P. Turner', which still exists in Kington). Philip Turner was the grandson of James Turner of Aymestrey Court, who died in 1806 and was famous for devoting his entire life to perfecting the Hereford breed of cattle (see MacDonald and Sinclair's *History of Hereford Cattle* and E. Heath Agnew's *History of Hereford Cattle and their Breeders*). My grandfather Philip bought the Island House, a lovely old Elizabethan building by the bridge in Kington which had formerly been owned by the Bevan family of Hay Castle. The Island House had a stone roof and, according to the description in *The Old Houses of Herefordshire*, a wonderful 15th-century staircase and 'acres of panelling'. He bought this house on his marriage to Emma, daughter of Edward Stanton Meyrick of Presteigne and London.

1

My grandparents Philip and Emma Turner with their three sons, Arthur, Cecil Philip (my father) and Elwyn, and Miss Lewis, at the Island House, Kington

Over the years the legend of the Black Hound of Hergest has been adapted, embroidered and distorted by many would-be authors and journalists after sensation and effect. I will attempt to tell it here in its simplest form. The basic tale of the curse of the Vaughans began before 1400. Hergest was a fortified stronghold then, with eight towers according to the bard Lewis Glyn Cothi. It was known for the gatherings that took place there – not just for feasting, but as a centre of bardic music and poetry.

The Lord of the Manor at that time was Tomas Ap Rosser, second son of Sir Roger Vaughan of Bredwardine. One fateful day, Tomas kidnapped a girl from Kington (a not unusual incident in those days) and locked her in an upstairs room for future amusement. In the middle of the feasting that evening, he remembered her and rushed up the stone stairway to bring her down. But she had gone, having escaped by climbing through the window and down the ivy. A brave country

Taken from the Red Book of Hergest.
The signature of Lewis Glyn Cothi *(as currently spelt)*
is at the foot of the right-hand column

Above: The Vaughan tomb in Kington Church
Below: The View from Stanner Rocks, drawn by Joseph Murray Ince

girl, she would not have run to her father's home in Kington, for it would then have been burnt down. (Kington in those times was the 'old Kington' by Castle Hill.) Climbing Hergest, she would have crossed the hill and headed down the other side towards Stanner Rocks, with some idea of hiding in a cave. If she could climb part of the sheer rock face, she would be safe from both hounds and riders.

In a terrible drunken rage by now, Vaughan shouted for his horse and his hounds (in those days they would have been wolfhounds, probably crossed with mastiffs). As he did so, he vowed that 'the devil could have his soul' if he did not get her back. This foolish oath was heard by his guests. It was night and the young men mounted and followed on, but as they descended the other side of Hergest Ridge a horse came back towards them, riderless, accompanied by cowed and whimpering hounds.

Peering in the moonlight at the bottom of Stanner Rocks they saw Vaughan lying there, with a huge black hound tearing at his throat. Nearby, the girl lay dead. Attempting to climb to safety, she had fallen and broken her neck. Vaughan was still alive, but he had been cursed by the Devil. The terrible hound disappeared before their horrified eyes. They carried Vaughan back to Hergest. He recovered only gradually, and was a changed man who would never speak of that night again.

Tomas, like his brothers and other members of his family, were supporters of Edward, Earl of March and the future Edward IV. Whilst there is no evidence that he fought at the battle of Mortimer's Cross in 1461, he received reward at the hands of Edward. In 1469, he died from wounds sustained at the Battle of Edgecote, like so many others from these parts. Lewis Glyn Cothi's bardic memorial to him translates thus:

> *Under the banner of the Lord of Hergest*
> *Was great contention, destruction and slaughter;*
> *Tomas ap Rosser with a sharp spear*
> *Was between two enraged parties –*
> *Tomas in bright polished armour*
> *Dealt out retaliation against his enemy ...*

So Tomas went down fighting bravely. His wife, Ellen Gethin, had his body brought back to Kington. Ellen herself was a fearsome and fearless lady who is said to have avenged the death of her brother by dressing up as a man to enter an archery contest at Llandewi Ystragenni and 'by turning suddenly on the murderer, put an arrow through his heart'.

Tomas and his wife have a beautiful alabaster tomb in the Vaughan Chapel of Kington Church. But Tomas' spirit could not rest there. The Devil in the shape of the Black Hound he had called up continued to hunt him through the centuries. Sometimes his spirit was seen alone, sometimes he was seen with the Hound, and sometimes just the awful cry of the Hound could be heard. Local people, of course, lived in fear, and horses and dogs in particularly reacted to this apparition.

One other legend clings on: the exorcism of Vaughan's spirit. It is so insistent that one wonders ... The place usually mentioned is Presteigne Church, but the century is uncertain. The participants are referred to as 'monks' so if the legend predates Henry VIII they could have been from Wigmore Abbey. (The nave of Presteigne Church was built by the monks of Wigmore.) The story goes that the monks reduced Vaughan's spirit to the size of a fly and imprisoned it in a snuffbox 'for a hundred years' and it was then thrown into the lake in front of Hergest Court. (The lake has been drained now but I remember it well. It is said that when it was first decided that the job was to be done, no local workman could be found who was prepared to take the risk.)

Incidentally, Bettws Disserth, in the extended parish of Glascwm, has not only a chalice of 1651 but a strange account of another very similar exorcism. Charles Lewis had been a miller in life, and his deeds were so sinful that they say his ghost went on haunting the village after his death. Parson Jones was the hero and held his ground although some of his assistant priests fainted. The evil spirit was finally reduced 'to the size of a fly' and imprisoned in a small box. His spirit was taken thus in procession to Llyncoedeggig and the box tied to a heavy iron bar and forced into the depths of the 'Quaking Mire'. If Arthur Conan Doyle ever heard this story, might it have inspired the Grimpen Mire of *The Hound of the Baskervilles*?

My father felt that all of this was more than just hearsay, and he gathered statements given to him by those who had had experience of the Hound, including my grandmother, and a Mrs Owens. These are included in Appendix 1.

Chapter 2
Arthur Conan Doyle – beginnings

'My dear fellow,' said Sherlock Holmes, as we sat on either side of the fire in his lodgings at Baker Street, 'Life is infinitely stranger than anything which the mind of man could invent. We would not dare to conceive the things which are really mere commonplace of existence.'

A Case of Identity

Arthur Ignatius Conan Doyle was born in Edinburgh at dawn on 22 May 1859 and thus in astrological terms he was a Gemini. This exactly fits his character – a lifelong contrast between a scientific mind of reason and a strong belief in spirituality and the dark forces of nature. Charles Altamont Doyle and Mary Josephine Foley gave their son names that had depths of meaning. He was named Arthur after King Arthur, of course; Ignatius for the saint's day on which his parents were married; and Conan after his mother's family, who were mixed Irish and English.

To say that the Doyle family were Irish leaves out the fact that they originated in England. Like many Catholic families, after many years in Ireland they returned to England. Charles Altamont Doyle (named after his father's one-time employer, the Marquess of Sligo) was the youngest of this very large and very gifted Irish family. They lived in London at 17 Cambridge Terrace and their father, John Doyle, was a noted and successful cartoonist who had moved from Ireland to London to be nearer Parliament and the political scene of action. The style of English political satire was changing from the rough and sometimes coarse 'old English' humour of Gillray and Rowlandson to a more cynical and urbane irony that exactly suited John Doyle's style, and under the professional name 'H.B' he was successful enough to support his large family and a substantial house.

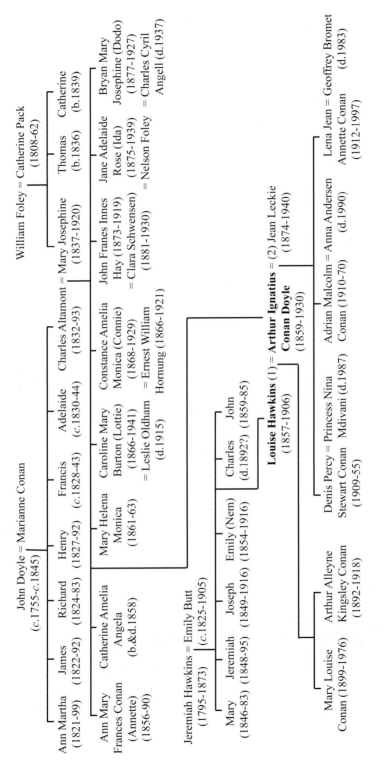

Arthur and Louise's family trees

Wishing his children to be educated at home, John Doyle took on their artistic training himself. Academic subjects were taught by a good tutor and professionals were brought in to teach extras such as dancing and fencing, essentials for the social scene. John's wife, Marianne Conan, contributed to the cultured atmosphere of the household; she was herself well educated and had French connections. All the children inherited artistic talent, and their father encouraged this in every way. Each weekend they would be expected to present a production, such as a scene of a play or a commentary on something observed during the week, and their awareness of events was always applauded. There were seven children in all: two girls, Annette and Adele, and five boys, James, Henry, Richard, Francis and Charles. Their education paid off. Henry became Director of the National Gallery of Ireland. James wrote *A Chronicle of England* and *The Official Baronage of England*, which is used for reference by the College of Arms to this day. Sadly, Francis, who his father believed had the most talent of them all, died as a young man.

The most widely known member of the family was probably Richard Doyle, Arthur's favourite 'Uncle Dicky', who died in 1883 after a long life. His wonderful sense of humour is seen in a folio of drawings called *Dick Kitkat's Book of Nonsense*, which is now in the Victoria and Albert Museum. His first published work was *The Eglinton Tournament*, published in 1840. He had a style and a decorative fancy all his own, and was invited to join the staff of *Punch* in 1843. In his wide portfolio were many pictures of fairies, elves and weird extra-terrestrial beings, and such figures made up the cornucopia of extraordinary designs that formed the surround of the cover of *Punch* and was used by the magazine, with only slight adjustments, for nearly a hundred years.

A frieze in the style of the Eglinton Tournament from Dick Doyle's Journal

Richard ('Dicky') Doyle

In 1850 Richard left *Punch*. As a Catholic he had disagreed strongly with the magazine's satirizing of the Pope. But by this time his incredible success had placed him high on the list of society hostesses; he even received invitations from royalty. When he illustrated Thackeray's *The Newcomes*, which was published in instalments in 1854 and 1855, he had found a writer whose humour was on a par with his own. It is rather like a shoreside version of Jerome K. Jerome's later work, *Three Men in a Boat*, telling the story of Brown, Jones and Robinson, three inept good friends who were always willing to attempt new ventures. Who could forget their Grand Tour of Europe? – Robinson's imprisonment in defence of his dog, Brown's mosquito-tortured night in Venice, the scant provisions for hygiene in a German hotel, the arrest of all three by Austrian police owing to the illegal shape of Brown's hat, Robinson falling off his horse at a prestigious German function, where they had been introduced in the local paper as 'Count Robinson', 'Sir Brown' and 'the Reverend Jones' ...

His observations as an illustrator of lively crowd scenes, published in 1864 in his *Bird's Eye View of Society*, were eagerly seized upon. His comments on the social scene were highly amusing and witty but never malicious. He has left hundreds of wonderful accurate drawings which must be a boon to producers of period plays of that time. He never married. He fell in love with Lady Airlie, one of the famous and beautiful Stanley sisters, but as she had already married, that was final. He was a 'loss to fatherhood', one of his friends remarked after looking at a Welsh-inspired sketch he had done for children; it showed a mother dragon smiling indulgently as she seated her brood for a see-saw on a Celtic stone.

The poem to his memory by Millais printed in *Punch* summed up his qualities perfectly:

> Turning o'er his own past pages
> Punch with tearful smile can trace
> Caustic satire, gentle grace ...
> ... masterpiece of mirth and truth.

No wonder Arthur loved him. It is said that when 'Uncle Dicky' had one of his attacks in the Atheneum Club, Arthur happened to be near by, and saved his uncle's life by swift action.

Charles Altamont Doyle, Arthur's father, also became an artist, but his story is not such a happy one. The discovery in 1977 of an illustrated diary of his revealed a sensitive, complex character, with enormous artistic ability, who destroyed himself and damaged his brain through alcohol until he was finally institutionalised at the asylum 'Sunnyside' for the rest of his life. The diary, found in a random lot of books in a sale in the New Forest, near where Arthur Conan Doyle lived before he died, was published by Michael Baker as *The Doyle Diary: The Last Great Conan Doyle Mystery* in 1978. The original diary, signed in his own hand by Charles Altamont Doyle and written while he was a patient at Blairerno Mental Hospital, began with the words 'Keep steadily in view that this book is ascribed wholly to the product of a MADMAN.'

The quality of Charles's art is variable because of the affliction, alcoholism, that took him to the care home. However, among the strange wit, the macabre addiction to fairies, threatening large birds and the ever recurring female faces showing the central hair parting and the prim little mouth of his wife Mary there are charming studies of foliage and flowers. The finest drawings, however, are his horses. This is difficult to understand until one searches back to the early life of his father to find that he had earned a very good reputation as a horse painter and portraitist, and received many commissions. He was quite sought after, and did well. He had received his schooling at a prestigious academy run by Samuel Whyte (Sheridan had been a pupil there) and afterwards gained a place at the Dublin Society's Drawing Academy. In 1814, at 17, he had exhibited three portraits of horses in the Hibernian Society of Artists. He rode and hunted himself, and had

Part of a page from Charles Altamont Doyle's diary

an inside knowledge and love of horses that shone through his work. This history, reflected in the love and accuracy of his son's depictions of horses, answers the question posed by the perfect and accurate line drawings in the book – the genes, or the skill, had been handed down to Charles. But something darker is evident in many of the drawings. His birds are fearsome, his elves evil, and 'The dreadful secret', showing a man on all fours, half dog, is the result of alcohol.

Some of the pencilled remarks in the book are badly rubbed but in one place he says: 'If in the whole Book you can find single evidence of lack of intellect or depraved taste, mark and record it against me.' There is now and then a flash of humour, like that of his brother Dicky. In the pencil annotations he wrote: 'I asked my paintings to be all sent to Mrs Doyle to submit to Publishers, but as I have never had a single book or Drawing acknowledged by her or *other relatives*, I can only conclude that they see no profit in them. It would be better that these books should be entrusted to the Lunacy Commissioners to show them the sort of intellect they think it right to imprison.' If it is truly the case that his wife Mary and his son Arthur did not acknowledge his writings, surely they were guilty of great cruelty. It might at least have given him some measure of self-respect. But the fact of his alcoholism was a guilty secret kept from the rest of the family as far as possible.

On his mother's side Arthur's family was again not truly Irish but they had plenty of land to their credit near Lismore, as back in 1748 his mother's grandfather, Thomas Foley, was agent at Lismore Castle for the Duke of Devonshire. The family did well, moving into the professional classes. In 1835, Thomas's son William, a doctor, married into the Pack family in Kilkenny, who were Protestants and had a proud line of military ancestors who figured with distinction in the Peninsula Campaign and at Waterloo. William's wife was Catherine Pack, who, with her sister, ran a boarding school for girls in Kilkenny. It would have been a finishing school as well, and it had been started by her mother. The Packs had the reputation of being a cultured family, and would have been well able to produce young ladies of quality. Catherine's grandfather was headmaster of Kilkenny College, Ireland's leading Protestant school.

The family would have been taken aback by Catherine's decision to marry and become a Catholic. Sadly, the love match came to an end in August 1841 when William died suddenly, still only in his thirties. Catherine had to do something now that her doctor husband was no more, and she started a new school, but it was not a success. She was by now a devout Catholic, and the times were bad then, with the potato famine starting. She had two young daughters, Mary and Catherine, to support, and was herself only 28, but she put her house up for sale and moved to Edinburgh. After obtaining a house in Clyde Street, near a Catholic church, she managed to set up an agency supplying British and foreign governesses to families and schools. It was a courageous move, but she needed another source of income as well, and decided to take a lodger. Through the Catholic church appeared the young Charles Altamont Doyle – only 17, but with a job in the Civil Service his father had arranged for him. The fact that Mary, Catherine's 12-year-old daughter, was sent to France for schooling in the same year had nothing to do with Charles's arrival. All the Packs had completed their education in France, so that they could learn the language, and the experience gave Mary a life-long love of French culture.

When she returned in 1854 aged 17 she was a trim petite girl. Charles was smitten, and marriage soon followed. The loss of her first two daughters at a very young age – Ann Mary died aged four and Catherine Amelia died in her first year – meant that her first-born son, Arthur, was of enormous importance to her. Having been educated in France, Mary had a fine brain. A woman of parts, according to Arthur she could feed a child and stir the porridge whilst reading the 'Revue des deux mondes'! She was a devout follower of Oliver Wendell Holmes, a Bostonian American who, as a doctor and profound writer, inspired Arthur to name his most famous fictitious character after him.

Mary had several more children after Arthur: Mary Helena (1861-63) (another early death), Caroline Mary (Lottie) (1865-1941), Constance Amelia (1868-1929), John Francis Innes (1873-1919), Jane Adelaide (Ida) (1875-1939) and Bryan Mary (Dodo) (1877-1927). A diminutive five foot one, she must have been exceedingly brave to face a life full of money worries and a drunken, sometimes insane, husband. To counteract this she retreated into a world of history, of mediaeval chivalry and mighty deeds of honour, and of 'royal' blood on both sides of the family which must be 'lived up to'. She was a wonderful storyteller. Arthur recounts in his memoirs how she would 'sink her voice to a whisper' at the most enthralling parts. Naturally he adored her, and would write to her nearly every week of his life.

Much has been written about these two interesting families; but here we just need enough to get a sense of the make-up and the genes that produced Arthur Conan Doyle. In keeping with the Catholic traditions of the family Arthur was sent to Stonyhurst; the uncles Doyle at Clifton Gardens in London paid the fees. Stonyhurst was chosen not only for its strict Catholic principles but also for the sound education given by the Jesuit teachers. In the autumn of 1868 Arthur entered the Junior part of Stonyhurst; this was the start of several years of education intended ultimately to equip him to assume responsibility for his parents' growing family.

He was not a happy pupil, but he did have access to all the books he wanted, even the boys' adventures of R.M. Ballantyne, Thomas Mayne Reid and, later, Jules Verne. His school reports did not improve after he moved to the Upper School two years later. Beatings were severe, but they only increased Arthur's determination not to be cowed. His school reports often included remarks like 'sulky temper' and 'lazy', although the evidence of his eager and retentive mind for science and astronomy makes the charge of laziness surprising. He was now deeply imbued with the Catholic faith; he rejoiced to his mother at the time of his Confirmation that his belief was all-consuming.

In his later years at the College, things went better. He had fishing as a pastime, which he loved, and in summer there was cricket, although he never achieved more than the 2nd XI (and the 2nd XV in rugby). He was still considered to be small for his age but he had discovered his ability to tell a good story and could hold his fellow pupils' interest for hours – so much so that he could demand payment in the form of cakes and fruit. He was aware now that he could keep people enthralled by the power of his imagination, a gift that stood him in good stead throughout his life. It is noted that during his final visit to his Doyle cousins in London his favourite place was the Chamber of Horrors in the Waxworks Museum of Madame Tussauds. In 1875 all that was on his mind was passing his University of London Matriculation. He was, with reason, proud when he passed; it had been an uphill climb.

After Arthur left school, the Rector suggested that he would benefit from a few months at Stella Matutina in the Austrian Alps, to polish up his German. Unfortunately the family in London who had paid readily for his education do not seem to have been willing to support this venture, and Arthur found himself without funds, as his own father had been 'ill' again and had 'resigned' from his civil service job with a mere pittance of a pension.

At home in Edinburgh, a certain Dr. Bryan Waller was becoming more and more influential in the Doyle household. His connection with the family had begun when he had taken part of the large house owned by the Doyles, which brought in very welcome rent money. He had the reputation of a well-connected medical doctor and a man of letters, through his uncle who had been a friend of Charles Dickens. Dr. Waller's growing influence in the household was disturbing to the young Arthur, even more so when he learned that his beloved mother would not be in Edinburgh to welcome him home, but had been invited to stay at Dr. Waller's large estate in Yorkshire. This set up an antipathy against Waller in Arthur's mind that lasted all his life.

It is unclear how Arthur eventually managed to afford to go to Austria (perhaps Dr. Waller paid, or perhaps the money was a present from his uncle) – but on his way home, he met his uncle Michael Conan in Paris. It seems that he found this elderly character very different to what he had expected and that his uncle was probably one of the first people who influenced him in the direction of spiritualism. Back in Edinburgh from the autumn of 1876, Arthur was a good brother to his younger siblings, telling stories to Innes and Ida. His father painted a little, drank a lot and must have been a strange but at this time fairly gentle figure, drifting round the home.

Arthur now knew without doubt that he wanted to become a medical doctor. He was extremely lucky to have the famous Edinburgh Medical School on his doorstep with all the faculties within walking distance. The school still had links with the Infirmary, which was established in 1741. In the Preliminary Examination, even after his sojourn in Austria, he did not do very well in German. The following year he was to tackle a broad spectrum of subjects – pharmacy, midwifery and vaccination, to name but a few. He interspersed his studies with spells as an assistant in General Practice, but this brought in no money, for in those days, when one was unqualified, one was merely fed, not paid.

He had some fine professors, including Sir Robert Christison and Sir Henry Littlejohn, Edinburgh's Medical Officer of Health. Littlejohn was bringing that horribly dirty city into the modern age, no easy task. He was also – and this interested Arthur greatly – introducing science into the law courts, through use of fingerprints and photography. Through Littlejohn Arthur met Dr. Joseph Bell, with whom he will always be associated, for it was Dr. Bell who inspired the way Sherlock Holmes found his evidence through assessing minute detail, a way which he made his own, and which we all know and admire.

Added to this, Charles Wyville Thomson was Arthur's tutor in Natural History, having just returned after three years at sea on *H.M.S. Challenger*. Arthur was also taught by Professor William Rutherford, on whom he later modelled Professor Challenger, the main character in *The Lost World*.

Even with such good tuition it is surprising that Arthur passed any exams at all, such were his worries at home. He was seeing his father's degeneration almost daily, from a gentle, artistic character into a sick, sly hulk of a man, ready to steal even household money for his addiction. It must have been distressing and at times heartbreaking to be a daily witness to this.

It was just as he was about to take his Prelims that his mother came up with the greatest surprise of all. Yet another baby arrived! Furthermore, the names of the newcomer were strange. She was named in St. Mary's Church on 6 April 1877 as Bryan Mary Julia Josephine. To make matters worse, she was registered by her mother as B. Mary Julia Josephine, which would seem to point to a certain desire on her mother's part not to acknowledge her first name.

This must have been a huge embarrassment to Arthur. Out of loyalty to his mother he would never have assumed her to have done anything wrong, but he must have felt the unspoken criticism and surprise of their friends. He himself would have accepted her explanation that the name was a simple message of thanks to Dr. Waller and his mother Julia for giving her a home at Masongill, and rescuing her from a husband who may, through his addiction, have become brutal at times.

It must be said that Arthur's mother and Dr. Waller had much in common; he was deeply read and could converse with her on her favourite subjects. Not a lot is known about him, but as far as Arthur's mother was concerned his generosity to her family must have been a lifeline. His family had large estates in Yorkshire and eventually he persuaded Arthur's mother to move her own family there, to a comfortable cottage. (Dr. Waller's mother Julia lived in the big house, Masongill.) The last Doyle daughter, Bryan, was only five when this move took place. From our perspective Dr. Waller is something of a mystery, and on his own instructions all of his personal papers were destroyed at his death. Arthur disliked him, possibly out of jealousy that he provided so much for his mother when, at the time, he could not do so himself. Nevertheless, how wonderful that Mary, Arthur's beloved 'Mam', she who had believed so completely in chivalry, had found herself a knight errant, albeit one twelve years younger than herself, who owned estates and money, and was happy to give her shelter! She was still only 46 and had been through so much. After having lived at Masongill for a time, although she was brought up in the Catholic faith, she turned Protestant, perhaps because it was easier to live the life of a quiet country gentlewoman with her children in that faith.

Arthur passed his exams and shortly afterwards went on a walking holiday on the island of Arran with his sisters Lottie and Connie; for a short while they were joined by their father, who was having one of his 'dry' spells. Back in Edinburgh, Arthur found time to enjoy himself. He played some cricket and some rugby, and gloried in 'fisticuffs', which was no more or less than a variant of bare-knuckled prize fighting left over from the last century, and hugely popular with students.

After a brief spell with a doctor in Sheffield, with whom he did not agree at all, Arthur was taken on by a Shropshire doctor. He also crossed swords frequently with this volatile man, but he worked there for over four months and found the glorious countryside and the Salopian air wonderful. The distant views of the Welsh hills evoked his Celtic dreaming, and he put on weight and grew taller. While Dr. Stuart was away he carried out a difficult emergency operation successfully and this increased his self-confidence.

Successfully completing his second year studies in Edinburgh, it came as a relief to him when his father was institutionalized at Blairerno House, north of Montrose, it having been said that by overturning a candle he had caused a fire at their home. Arthur got a job in a practice run by Dr. Reginald Radcliff Hoare in Birmingham, which paid him a salary of £2 a month and would count towards his finals. Dr. Hoare had a big inner city practice so the days were varied. Arthur got on well with the family, and was able to find time for some writing of his own, even having one story accepted by 'Chambers' for £3.

Having achieved his ambition of becoming an official university lecturer in pathology, Dr. Bryan Waller had entered into a spirited interchange of letters about German Idealism with Arthur, who enjoyed the ideas and philosophy, but always felt that in becoming involved with Dr. Waller in this way he was being disloyal to his mother.

At this point, by chance, Arthur was taken on by the 575-ton whaling ship *Hope*, due to sail from Peterhead, Aberdeenshire on 27 February, 1880, simply because a friend of his, a fellow student, had been unable to go. He would be paid £2 10s a week and after the voyage was over, he would get a share of the money from the sale of whale oil. The ship's captain turned out to be an extremely interesting character, a veteran of whaling with a homespun philosophy, and the chief engineer similarly had a tale to tell. Arthur had taken several books including his current favourite, Macaulay's *Essays*, and he kept a diary in which he wrote descriptions of the frozen Arctic wastes, and made pen and ink sketches as well. The fresh air, the outdoor life, the good and simple food with plenty of fresh fish, not to mention a generous supply of wine, meant that he muscled up and generally commanded the respect of the crew (ranging from ages 17 to 70) with his ability in 'fisticuffs' to black a few eyes.

One very important part of this voyage was the fact it gave him authentic background. Arthur was always very keen on backgrounds to his stories, and it may be this that gets us straight into the telling of his tales. We feel we are really there. The story he wrote based on this journey several years later, 'The Captain of the Polestar', comes across as totally authentic. Arthur shows no pity or sentimentality in his account of the clubbing to death of hundreds of young seals. It was called a 'cull' and was treated as such. On this voyage Arthur came of age.

He returned for a while to Dr. Hoare's practice in Birmingham and must have kept the family spellbound for hours with his stories. He had become a man at sea; now it was time to concentrate on the work he still needed to do to qualify. To his credit he foreswore alcohol for several months, aware that drink had ruined his father's life. Returning to Edinburgh for his finals, he found that his mother was living in a different house, one leased to Dr. Waller. The family were nearly all together, except for his father, who was still at Blairerno.

Arthur passed with honours, a very creditable performance. Now he decided to visit his mother's relations in Ireland, the Foleys, at Lismore. He spent the summer there, and as the family lived a very elegant country life, he enjoyed himself enormously. It was here he met his first serious girlfriend, nicknamed 'Elmo'. There were several others, but this one remained quite important in his life – for a time, at least.

Once the summer was over, with the thought of new adventure in mind, he applied for a job as a ship's surgeon on the *Mayumba*, which was departing for West Africa the following week with 30 passengers. He sailed from Liverpool on 22 October. He didn't like the mix of passengers, and must have been fair game for the flirtations of the women on board. The Bay of Biscay crossing was rough, and once they reached the African coast Arthur immediately hated it. The ports were smelly and dirty and Arthur succumbed to fever. Realising that he was drinking too much, he cut down, again thinking of his father. In the course of his travels he met an interesting character, an elderly black man who was travelling to take up his post in Monrovia as United States Consul in Liberia. With him Arthur had interesting discussions and learned a lot about the condition of Africa.

The ship returned in January 1882. Although the journey had added to his experiences, Arthur's dislike of the tropics meant it was unlikely he would return. However, he had again picked up enough authentic background to write several stories of the sea.

At this point, Arthur was considering what his future should be when he received a telegram from his friend and former co-student George Budd (in the *Stark Munro Letters*, a semi-autobiographical work, Arthur calls him Cullingworth). A man of irrepressible energy and 'a temper nothing less than infernal' who constantly walked the tightrope between genius and downright illegal practice, he came of a good family in Devon, and must have been an eternal headache for them. He had wired Arthur once before, assuring him of riches galore if he would join forces with him, but luckily (given that it was likely to be a hare-brained scheme) the wire arrived just when Arthur was off to sea on his Arctic voyage. Now, however, intrigued in spite of himself, he thought it might be the time to join his friend, who was in Plymouth and apparently making a fortune.

He found Budd seemingly very prosperous, with an elegant house and patients flocking to his surgery. He offered Arthur the right to take his surgical cases and to put up his own brass plate; it all seemed plain sailing. With Budd, however, things never happened calmly, and it was no time at all before their relationship blew up with Wagnerian intensity. Budd even destroyed Arthur's brass plate with a hammer! The reason for the row was that Budd had been reading Arthur's letters from his mother, and as that lady had always mistrusted him, it was the end of the road for the partnership. So once more, with no money, good qualifications and nothing else, Arthur faced the future.

Chapter 3
The turning point: Arthur meets Louise

'From a drop of water,' said the writer, 'a logician could infer the possibility of an Atlantic or a Niagara without having seen or heard of one or the other. So all life is a great chain, the nature of which is known whenever we are shown a single link of it.'

> *from* The Book of Life, *an article by Holmes quoted in* A Study in Scarlet

Arthur Conan Doyle faced a crucial decision. Where was he going to go? At least the experience with Budd, although short-lived, had shown him that building up a practice was possible. He just had to decide which part of the country he was going to favour with his presence. Searching for a town in which to start his career as a doctor, Arthur kept several points in mind. First of all, he wanted to live on the coast – he had grown attached to Plymouth even in the short time he had been there – and the town would have to have a thriving population and a stirring history.

Thus he went to Portsmouth, a town of three parts. First there was the Dockyard, ancient and full of history – events there could be traced back to King Rufus. Then there was the Commercial Road at the back of the town, the roughest area, with a thriving mass of poor and not so poor clerks and artisans of every description. And the third area was around Southsea Common, favoured by holiday makers and retired people, with its bandstand, the hotels along the front, and the modest, well-kept homes of those who, even in their last years, could not be parted from the sight of the sea.

As an aspiring writer, Arthur would certainly have known that Portsmouth was the birthplace of Charles Dickens (he was born in

Commercial Road, the son of a clerk in the Dockyard) and that Rudyard Kipling had been brought up by his foster-parents in Campbell Road. Other names linked with the town included George Meredith, born in 1828, and Isambard Kingdom Brunel.

Upon finding a house which he felt would suit him, Arthur managed to obtain its tenancy by mentioning his uncle, who had recently been made a C.B. (Companion of the Bath). It did the trick, and with very few pounds to his name he found himself in possession of a sound Victorian house with good-sized rooms, a basement and attic rooms. In his descriptions of his meagre second-hand possessions (he didn't even have a bedcover at first), he never complained. His account of this period in his life in the *Stark Munro Letters* is very humorous; for example, he describes polishing his own brass plate at night so that he shall *not* be seen not to have a servant! The *Stark Munro Letters* were published several years later, but there is no reason to suppose that they do not give a more or less accurate account. He is amused his house lies between a church and a pub – 'two opiates', he wrote, 'one for the body and one for the soul'.

On the train down to Portsmouth on the very day of his arrival in 1882, he found himself sharing a carriage with two ladies, a mother and daughter, and also the son of the family, who was in his early twenties. During the journey there was an unwelcome incident; the young man suddenly had an epileptic fit, a symptom of his meningitis. Arthur helped and reassured them, and was most impressed by the way the mother dealt with the attack and calmly administered the bromide she always carried with her. He also noted that he felt strongly attracted to the daughter, and especially the sweetness of her attitude to her mother. The mother explained that they were living in Queen's Gate, adjacent to the Osborne Road. She gave him her card, and no doubt he explained that as he was at that moment of no fixed abode, he could not reciprocate with a card of his own, but would certainly call on them once he was established.

One of the first friends he made in Portsmouth was Dr. William Royston Pike, who lived nearby, at the top end of Yarborough Road. Dr. Pike was ten years older that Arthur, but also Edinburgh-trained. Far from resenting the arrival of another doctor in the neighbourhood, he was most welcoming – in fact it was he who suggested to Arthur it would be no good offering free consultation to his future patients (as Dr. Budd had done in Plymouth), for the local people in Portsmouth had made their own way in life and never wanted to be seen as receiving 'charity'. This was sound advice.

It is thought by some biographers that at this time Arthur asked his mother if she would send his brother Innes down to him. If he did, it was perhaps because he wanted to get the ten-year-old Innes away from the influence of Dr. Waller, his distrust of whom was now very profound. His mother agreed to send Innes and, certainly as far as Arthur was concerned, the arrangement was a great success. This enchanting description gives some idea of the relationship: 'My little brother ... came down – and the best of companions he is! He shares the discomforts of my little menage in the cheeriest spirit, takes me out of my blacker humours, goes long walks with me, is interested in all that interests me (I always talk to him exactly as if he were my own age) and is quite ready to turn his hand to anything, from boot blacking to medicine carrying. His one dissipation is cutting out of paper, or buying in lead (on the rare occasions when we find we have a surplus), an army of little soldiers. I have brought a patient into the consulting room, and found a torrent of cavalry, infantry and artillery pouring across the table. I have been myself attacked, and sat silently writing, and have looked up to find fringes of sharp-shooters pushing up towards me, columns of cavalry on my flank, while a battery of pea muzzle-loaders on the ridge of my medical dictionary has raked my whole position – with the round smiling face of the general behind it all. I don't know how many regiments he has on a peace footing; but if serious trouble were to break out, I am convinced that every sheet of paper in the house would spring to arms.' This passage mirrors exactly the character that Innes was to become.

For 'the Mam' to have sent her ten-year-old son to share her doctor son's impecunious start to life in an unknown garrison town was a risk. She could see, however, that to be the only boy left in the fold with her would have been the wrong sort of life for young Innes. The move seems to have suited him; he was delighted to watch the ships, the Marines, the parades and the general excitement of a huge naval port.

A circle of friendship was now forming around Arthur that was to affect his whole life. Dr. William Royston Pike was family doctor to

Mrs. Hawkins and her daughter, and also her son, who was afflicted by meningitis and epilepsy. He introduced them to Arthur, and it was only then that Arthur realised that he had met them a few months before, on the train. Somewhere in his suit pocket was the card Mrs. Hawkins had given him. They happened to live fairly close to him, at No. 2 Queen's Gate, a nice part of Southsea facing the common and the sea. They had perhaps taken these lodgings because Mrs. Hawkins, after years with a very much older husband and several children, was taking the opportunity to take things a little more easily. Arthur remembered them perfectly (particularly the daughter), as he later recounted in the *Stark Munro Letters*), and he was just a little affronted that they didn't seem to remember him! – but it emerged that this was because when they first met he had a beard.

When Innes came to live with Arthur, it was only natural that Louise would include him in walks with her own brother. This would have been a great help to Arthur, who was trying to find time when free of the surgery to get on with writing. At this time he managed to publish a story called 'The Winning Shot' which earned £3. He now had a housekeeper, a Mrs. Smith, who was a godsend. Not only did she run the house efficiently; she was the perfect psychologist with visiting patients, making them feel that although the doctor was incredibly busy, he would make time 'just to see them'. Arthur further increased his circle of friends, and therefore of patients, by playing cricket and joining the bowls club. In the meantime, on his walks with Louise and her brother, Innes was forming a bond he would keep all his life. Louise was young enough to enjoy flying a kite. They marvelled at the parades of the Navy and the Royal Marines and even sailed a model boat themselves on the lake. Soon, now that Innes' move was clearly going to be long-term, Arthur arranged for his brother to attend a little day school nearby in the mornings.

Arthur's romance with Elmo, the girl he knew in Ireland, was now over. The striking Miss Elmore Weldon was heiress to a fortune, which of course had interested Arthur's mother, and she had encouraged the friendship strongly, in the hope that the two would marry. However, when Arthur and Elmo met again in London the flame had died, and there was no more talk from his mother about it. Clearly his thoughts were now centred on Louise, and a much stronger love.

He wrote a very successful story, 'J. Habukak Jephson's Statement', which was accepted and brought in 29 guineas, but on the whole he wasn't having much success in getting his writing published. However, he was invited to Smith Elders' end of year dinner at the Ship Tavern, Greenwich, and met George du Maurier (of *Trilby* fame) and F. Anstey, who had just written the best seller *Vice Versa*.

He joined the Portsmouth Library and Scientific Society in 1883 and was asked to give a talk for them. He had an audience of 250, so his ability to tell a story was getting noticed. He spoke about his Arctic voyage, and to illustrate the talk he managed to borrow several good specimens of northern birds from a taxidermist. It was at the Society that he made the acquaintance of Major General Alfred Drayson, who had been a surveyor in the Royal Artillery and recently a Professor at the Royal Military Academy in Woolwich. Like Arthur, he had an interest in the paranormal.

In January 1885 Mrs. Hawkins, Louise and John's mother, approached their family physician, Dr. Pike, with a problem that was becoming more difficult to handle ever day. The Hawkins lived in charming lodgings with several other paying guests. This was quite the 'done' thing then, far more than it would be now, with guests booking up semi-permanently, or very often for a year at a time. John was now badly afflicted with meningitis. The attacks were increasing, and the noise he made caused disturbance and distress to the other guests, particularly at night. The thought had come into both his mother's and Dr. Pike's minds that Arthur, with a large house, an empty bedroom and a competent housekeeper who was not in the least averse to the idea of 'one extra', would benefit from the little increase of income a paying guest would give, while the lad would have constant access to medical help, and if he had an attack at night he would not inconvenience a large household. Arthur was always interested in illnesses that attacked the mind, and would be able to treat the case intensively, observing any change as it happened. And so the arrangement was made.

On 24 March, Dr. Pike came round in the evening. Arthur had asked his advice, as the patient had quite a high temperature. Arthur told Dr. Pike he was administering bromide of potassium which usually seemed to be effective, but that he had added a little choral to the dose. Choral had the reputation of sometimes having a toxic action that could produce irregularities. Dr. Pike agreed with everything Arthur was doing, and John's temperature was indeed falling. He was now in a deep sleep, and he was still sleeping when Arthur looked in last thing. When the housekeeper, Mrs. Smith, took up the patient's arrowroot in the morning, it was a terrible shock to her to find him dead.

Arthur of course was horrified, but he could not help noticing the wonderful serenity which had transformed the boy's features, which the day before had been contorted with suffering. This was the sort of thing that redoubled his interest in spiritualism and ideas of a world beyond our own. The dreadful part was that he now had to go round and tell Mrs. Hawkins and Louise that John had died. They must have feared that one day this would happen, but Arthur was very impressed with their dignity at such a time. He wrote, 'In their womanly unselfishness their sympathy was all for me and the shock which I had suffered! I found myself being turned from the consoler to the consoled.'

Arthur took charge of all the necessary formalities for them. The grave is in the Highland Road Cemetery, marked by a carved hand on which is engraved 'From darkness into light'. When Arthur returned home after the funeral, a 'burly man with bushy side whiskers' was standing on the doorstep saying he had 'come to inquire about the death of a young man resident in your house'. The unpleasant fact was that the Council had received an anonymous letter that very morning about the young man who had died, asserting that the circumstances were suspicious. When Arthur told his visitor that it was he who had signed the death certificate, the man looked even more suspicious. However, as soon as Arthur told him that Dr. Pike had seen the patient the night before, it was a different matter. 'That is final, Dr. Doyle,' his interviewer said, shutting his notebook with a snap. 'I will of course see Dr. Pike, and if his opinion agrees with yours, I can only apologise for this intrusion.'

Although the matter was resolved so quickly, it must have been a dreadful shock to Arthur. It would also have made him see the importance of evidence in the assessment of any catastrophic happening. No one ever found out who had written the horrible letter.

Arthur's friendship with Louise was strengthening and he was appreciating the sweetness of her character more and more. Another link between them was that her eldest brother, Ebenezer, had had a nervous breakdown and was in a mental hospital in Gloucester. He had great artistic talent and had been successful at art college. Mrs. Hawkins never gave up on him and had him with her from time to time, and it seems that by 1891 he was living with her in Portsea. Of course, Arthur had troubles with his father, who was in and out of hospital with dementia, so both families had anxieties with mental illness. This gave Arthur and Louise the freedom to be perfectly frank with each other. There was no need for subterfuge, no feelings of guilt or a sense of family secrets undisclosed.

Arthur was quite definitely falling in love with this beautiful, quiet and serene girl whom Fate had brought into his life. Why else would he write the poem 'Saucy Kate'?

> Saucy Kate was the belle of the town
> And Oh! she laughed as she tossed her head
> Shall I take the first who comes? she said
> What, though John be a comely lad
> Such suitors as this may ever be had
> I may very well wait
> Said Saucy Kate
> For suitors like John may ever be had!

There are more verses, and Kate rejects two more suitors, only to end up unmarried! A rather obvious warning from Arthur, and perhaps a little unchivalrous. He asked Louise's mother for her blessing on their marriage, and it was given. All his life Arthur held his mother-in-law in the highest esteem. In a letter written in 1905 when she was ill, he wrote, 'What a singularly amicable and gentle creature she has ever been.' The idea at first was Louise and Arthur would wait for six months before getting married, but in the event it wasn't quite that long. Arthur makes it clear in the *Stark Munro Letters* that he did not know Louise had a tiny private income. He had to admit that it would help, but wanted to record that it was not the reason for the marriage. Arthur's mother came down to Portsmouth to 'vet' the intended wife, and she approved wholeheartedly and congratulated her son on his choice. As for Innes, he had adored Louise from the first time they met, and remained her loyal admirer all his life.

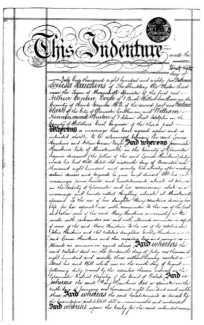

Indenture showing settlement
on Louisa Hawkins

When his mother came down to Portsmouth Arthur must have breathed a sigh of relief that she approved of Louise and got on well with Mrs. Hawkins. One thing which appealed to her was that one of the Doyle family, Arthur's Uncle James, had married a Jane Henrietta Hawkins of Tredunnock, Monmouthshire. The Hawkins family had deep roots in the part of the country that straddles the Welsh Border from Monmouth to Gloucester and up the Severnside. They can be traced back to 1608 and always figure in the pedigree as yeoman landowners or squires. Louise's grandfather bought Murcott Manor Farm from the Atkyns family, and her father Jeremiah farmed at Elmore, Gloucestershire, though in the census of 1861 we find him retired and living at Leckhampton. In June 1845 he had married Emily Butt (also from a farming family) at Gloucester. He was thirty years older than his wife. There were five children: Jeremiah, Mary, Emily, Louise and John, all born near Monmouth. When their father died in 1873, he left a most detailed will concerning the properties and small farms he owned. His widow found that there was just sufficient income for her to live on the proceeds in watering places which might benefit John, her epileptic son, which is why they ended up in Southsea.

It was early autumn when I recently went to find the two hill farms, Clyro Bettws and Whitehall Farm, that belonged to Louise Hawkins. The view across to the Black Mountains was of such beauty and changing light and shadow that it would have been easy to forget that it was a hard living there in the 1890s. In his diaries Francis Kilvert frequently mentioned the tiny church of Bettws Clyro which Kilvert called a 'chapel'. On St. Valentine's Eve 1870, Septuagesima Sunday, he walked up from Clyro, its parent church, and noted:

The weather fearful, violent E. wind and the hardest frost
we have had yet. I went to Bettws in the afternoon wrapped
in two waistcoats, two coats, a muffler and a mackintosh ...
When I got to the Church my beard and whiskers were so
stiff with ice I could hardly open my mouth and my beard
was frozen. There was a large christening party from Llwgn
Gwilwym – the baby was baptised in ice which was broken
and floating about in the font.

Another time, on Sunday 3 September 1871 he notes:

I went to Bettws in light rain and preached extempore on
the Good Samaritan from the Gospel of the day. A red cow
with a foolish white face came up to the window by the
desk, and stared in while I was preaching.

The last time Kilvert preached from here on Sunday 25 August 1872
before he left the parish for good, he broke down and burst into tears.
'I could not help it – it was a sad, sad day.'

Holy Trinity, Bettws Clyro by Ursula Cooper

If Louise ever visited her properties at this time with her father, she would only have been a young girl. It is doubtful, and we have no record that she ever came here with Arthur. When they were first married they would not have had the time or the money, and later, Arthur was even busier, and Louise herself was ill.

It is nothing short of extraordinary that in all the biographies written about Arthur Conan Doyle, hardly anything has been mentioned about the Hawkins family until in 2004 Georgina Doyle's book *Out of the Shadows* was published. It is now realised that considerable 'weeding' was carried out by Arthur's second wife, so that little would be left in the family documents to give any idea of the importance to him and depth of love of his first marriage. Arthur wrote to his mother, 'the Mam', nearly every week of his life. The only time there is a gap is during the first two years of his marriage – the very time when the letters would have been most fulsome in praise of his new wife. In *A Life in Letters*, edited by Jon Lellenberg, Daniel Stashower and Charles Foley (2007), the editors note that: 'there followed some of the happiest years with Louisa, whom Arthur called "Touie"'. Surely letters written by Arthur to his mother in this period must be missing.

It is sad that jealousy could have had such an effect. Perhaps it built up during the long wait until the second Lady Conan Doyle could appear in public as Arthur's legal wife. It is only now that we can see that it was his first marriage that inspired him to write his best work, including the invention of Sherlock Holmes, as well as producing two strong, healthy and intelligent children, both of whom did good in this world.

Chapter 4
Marriage and the Muse

*I have seen too much not to know that the impression of a woman may
be more valuable than the conclusion of an analytical reasoner.*

Sherlock Holmes, from 'The Man with the Twisted Lip'

Arthur and Louise were married in Yorkshire at St. Oswald's church,
Thornton-in-Lonsdale, near Dr. Waller's home. Louise's mother, Mrs.
Emily Hawkins, had already journeyed to the solicitors in Monmouth
in order to set up the rather lengthy legal proceedings for the marriage
settlement. Louise's sister Mary had died in New Zealand in 1883,
and now John, her brother, had also passed away. The witnesses at the
wedding were Bryan Waller, Emily Hawkins, Julia Waller, J.F. Innes,
H. Doyle (he was only 12), Mary J. Doyle and Constance A.M. Doyle.
It was a very quiet family wedding, as Louise's brother had died only
five months earlier, so technically she was still in mourning.

The announcement in the *Hampshire Telegraph*, dated 8 August 1885,
was as follows: 'Doyle-Hawkins. On the 6th inst. At Thornton-in-
Lonsdale Parish Church, by the Rev. S.R. Stable, Arthur Conan Doyle
MD of Bush Villas, Southsea, to Louise, youngest daughter of the late
Jeremiah Hawkins Esq. of Minsterworth, Gloucestershire'. The same
announcement was repeated a week later in the *Monmouthshire Beacon* on
Saturday August 15th so that the many friends of the Hawkins family
in that area could hear the news.

The marriage agreement showed clearly that amongst her other
properties Louise owned two farms 'in the County of Radnor', Clyro
Bettws and Whitehall Farm. These properties are surrounded by estates
belonging to the Baskerville family. One cannot help thinking that this
most historic and romantic of names must now have been firmly lodged
in Arthur's mind for future use.

After the wedding Arthur played a lot of cricket both for the 'Old Boys' of Stonyhurst and later in Ireland, so the weather must have been lovely. This might possibly have been a clever plan to make sure his mother and Louise would be spending enough time together to get to know each other really well. Louise did go to Ireland with him, however; both of them loved walking.

When they came back to Portsmouth, their married life together appears to have been very happy indeed. For Arthur there was no significant jolt between being a bachelor and a young husband, except that he was now cared for, and had a well run home. Louise was an excellent manager, as well as being a competent cook herself. Her little domestic team had grown; besides Mrs. Smith, the redoubtable housekeeper who had been so loyal and helpful to Arthur, there was Mrs. Collins, an old retainer who had worked for Louise and her mother for years, and a new cook. There was also a 'morning maid' who helped Mrs. Smith (at one shilling a week), and no doubt on wash days there would have been a washerwoman (turning a mangle took time and strength). It was lucky that Arthur had rented a large house when he arrived in Southsea! However, just at the time when Arthur's letters to his mother would surely have been full of praise of his new life, no letters have been found. This is the only period of his life from which no letters to his mother have been found. The suggestion must be that they were destroyed by his second wife.

To suggest that Arthur married only for convenience does not do him justice and makes him appear shallow. It is not as though Louise was a plain and awkward woman. To judge from her portrait she was quite beautiful, with luxuriant hair piled up, arresting blue-grey eyes and a soft mouth. Above all she had a sweetness of nature, a calm influence and a quiet Anglican faith. At her bedside she kept a copy of Thomas à Kempis' *The Imitation of Christ*, which she read each evening. Certain passages were well marked. Her Christian faith never varied, and was not even shaken by her later illness. A better match could not have been found for this ambitious, volatile young doctor on the brink, as we know now, of fame.

Musing in the *Stark Munro Letters*, Arthur wrote of his wife, 'She is the best, the kindest, the sweetest little woman in England' – and 'How good is that saying of some Russian writer that he who loves one woman

Louise Conan Doyle, painting attributed to Julia Pocock
(courtesy of Mrs. Georgina Doyle)

knows more of the whole sex that he who has passing relationships with a thousand?' and further on 'I did not know how easy it is to be noble, when some one else takes it for granted that you will be so ...' Are not these the thoughts of a man who loves deeply?

They made a number of good friends in Portsmouth, some influential, and took their place in social life; of course, this was beneficial for Arthur as a doctor. Among them was Henry Percy Boulnois, Borough Engineer of Portsmouth, and he and his wife remained life-long friends of Arthur's.

Several years later, when the Doyles' daughter Mary was a teenager and they lived at Undershaw in Surrey, Mary recorded quite an amusing incident. Arthur had invited a famous author, Helen Mathers, to dinner and then forgotten all about it! Halfway through the meal their guest arrived, resplendent in pink evening dress and pearls. Arthur was terribly embarrassed and agitated, but Louise 'took charge of the situation with a calmness and charming dignity all her own ... She put everyone at their ease by her own refusal to be embarrassed or appear to be taken aback. We all took our cue from her, and started talking naturally, and soon the position was restored.' The perfect hostess!

Arthur now started to write *A Study in Scarlet*, which he described as 'the scarlet thread running through the colourless skein of life'. From many setbacks, there gradually emerged the character of Sherlock Holmes, and the staunch Dr. Watson with his Army experiences (based, it is thought, on a doctor neighbour in Portsmouth).

Arthur tackled the question of religion in the *Stark Munro Letters*: 'You will wonder, perhaps, how we get on, my wife and I, in the matter of religion? Well, we both go our own ways. Why should I proselytize? I would not, for the sake of abstract truth, take away her childlike Faith which serves to make life easier, and brighter to her!' and later, 'As for my wife I would as soon think of breaking in upon her innocent prayers, as she would of carrying off the works of philosophy from my study table.'

At this stage Arthur made no mention on the subject of spiritualism, but a year or two later he was being drawn towards it. Louise did not try to go against his interest – in fact, she joined in with one 'round table' séance. Her approach was to try to channel his ability and enthusiasm through his knowledge of science and his experience of the diseases of the mind (knowledge added to by the condition of his father, who was growing daily more insane) .

Arthur's *Stark Munro Letters* seem to contain his deepest thoughts at this time, even more than his diary. Because of this, the following is of great importance. After a heated argument with a vicar in Portsmouth who called on him, Arthur wrote his thoughts as follows:

> I am only bigoted against bigotry, and that I hold to be as legitimate as violence to the violent. When one considers what effect the perversion of the religious instinct has had during the history of the world; the bitter wars, Christian and Mohammedan, Catholic and Protestant; the persecutions, the torturings, the domestic hatreds, the petty spites, with all creeds equally blood guilty, one cannot but be amazed that the concurrent voice of mankind has not placed bigotry at the very head of the deadly sins. It is surely a truism to have brought the same misery upon mankind.
>
> I cannot be bigoted, my dear boy, when I say from the bottom of my heart that I respect every good Catholic and every good Protestant, and that I recognise that each of these forms of truth has been a powerful instrument in the hands of that inscrutable Providence which rules all things. Just as in the course of history one finds that the most far-reaching and admirable effects may proceed from a crime; so in religion, although a creed be founded upon an entirely inadequate conception of the Creator and His ways, it may none the less be the very practical thing for the people and age which have adopted it. But if it is right for those to whom it is intellectually satisfying to adopt it, it is equally so for those to whom it is not, to protest against it, until by this process the whole mass of mankind gets gradually leavened, and pushed a little bit further on their slow upward journey.
>
> Catholicism is the more thorough. Protestantism is the more reasonable. Protestantism adapts itself to modern civilisation. Catholicism expects civilisation to adapt itself to it. Folk climb from one big branch to the other big branch,

and think they have made a prodigious change, when the main trunk is rotten beneath them, and both must in their present forms be involved sooner or later in a common ruin. The movement of human thought, though slow, is still in the direction of truth, and the various religions which man sheds as he advances (each admirable in its day) will serve, like buoys dropped down from a sailing vessel, to give the rate and direction of his progress.

But how do I know what is truth, you ask? I don't, but I know particularly well, what isn't. And surely that is something to have gained. It isn't true that the great central Mind that planned all things is capable of cruelty or injustice. These are human attributes; and the book which ascribes them to the Infinite must be human also.

Taking this theme further, he goes on:

When first I came out of the faith in which I had been reared, I certainly did feel for a time as if my life-belt had burst. I won't exaggerate and say that I was miserable and plunged in utter spiritual darkness. Youth is too full of action for that. But I was conscious of a vague unrest, of a constant want of repose, of an emptiness and hardness which I had not known in life before. I had so identified religion with the Bible that I could not conceive them apart. When the foundations proved false, the whole structure came rattling about my ears. And then good Carlyle came to the rescue; and partly from him, and partly from my own broodings, I made a little hut of my own, which had kept me snug ever since and has served to shelter a friend or two besides.

Louise was always wise enough not to interfere with the time Arthur needed to write, or with his philosophies. She had her own interests too; for example, she was an excellent pianist. Louise's mother, Mrs. Hawkins, did not live with them, but when she was at her own home nearby, of course she visited frequently, and sometimes Louise went with her to help when she had her son to stay with her, usually taking him to a watering place like Bath or Eastbourne. She never gave up on him and as he was now hardly ever prone to violent attacks, the mental hospital in Gloucester allowed him out more and more. It seems that his father, when alive, had always had an adverse influence on him, and that they had often quarrelled badly. His mother's patience and devotion were rewarded for from 1891 it is recorded that he was living with her permanently until his death.

Lottie, Arthur's sister from Portugal, came to stay and formed an immediate friendship with Louise although there was a difference of nine years in age. Later she went to Paris with Louise's sister 'Nem' for a short holiday, escorted by Arthur. Louise did not go as she was pregnant. Some biographers infer that as two years had elapsed by this time Louise may have had difficulty in conceiving. However, it is a fact that the first year or two after marriage is the ideal space for a husband and wife to get to know each other before beginning that very different relationship involving a child – and at least there is no doubt at all that the baby was conceived in wedlock.

It is also sometimes suggested that Innes went away to school as soon as Louise and Arthur married, because he was not wanted. This was very far from the truth. He urgently needed some good schooling, for the little day school he had attended at Portsmouth (though not for long) had not given him the grounding he would need for his Entrance exams to Woolwich. It was arranged, therefore, that he would go to Richmond Grammar School in Yorkshire (which had been Dr. Waller's old school), which would enable him to spend the school holidays at Masongill with his mother. He loved walking the Yorkshire Moors, and later Dr. Waller gave him a gun, on condition he used it sensibly. No doubt Arthur, with his antipathy towards Brian Waller, did not like the arrangement much, but for the boy's sake he could only agree. When the time came for Innes to take his entry exams he did not pass, so he returned to Arthur and Louise at Southsea for a year or two, and after some intensive 'cramming' at Portsmouth Grammar School, he was at last successful. At this time Portsmouth Grammar School had a reputation for being strict and sometimes harsh, but, perhaps glad to be back with Arthur and Louise, Innes was able to apply himself seriously. Thus began a fine career serving his country.

A Study in Scarlet proved very difficult to place, and in the end Arthur received only a pittance for it. It is obvious that Louise was of the greatest help and support to him. It was his custom to read his writing of the day aloud to her in the evenings, and when it was a murder mystery, he was impressed that her 'womanly intuition' would often lead to the solution of the plot. Louise now knew all about his leanings towards the occult, but urged that when it came to the solving of crime, scientific analysis was also needed.

At this time criminology was developing swiftly, with the help of science. Up till this point, the detection of crime had failed to keep up with modern scientific methods. This had not mattered so much in the past, as crime itself had been slow-moving, but now crime was becoming much more sophisticated, and detection methods had to catch up. Francis Galton, Charles Darwin's cousin, had just given an extraordinary talk, the Rede Lecture at Cambridge in May 1884 on 'The Measurement of Human Faculty'. Describing his stand at that year's International Health Exhibition in Kensington as his 'anthropometric laboratory', he gathered physical data, including fingerprints, from any willing passerby.

As we know, Arthur had a wonderful ability to tell a good story and hold the reader's attention. Now he combined this with a character who would, with his scientific knowledge combined with shrewd observation, be able to solve any crime. As he took flesh, as it were, this main character became a collector of violins, a philosopher, and an expert in chemistry. His friend and foil would be a medical doctor, someone with military experience. As a contrast to the complex main character, he would not be of supreme intelligence, but would make up for this by his courage, his expertise with a revolver, his integrity and his loyalty. Above all he would be a true servant of the British Empire – a characteristic which appealed to the reader at once. Louise listened, suggested and commented, and those evenings together brought forth two characters: Sherlock Holmes and Doctor Watson.

Chapter 5
Malvern Chase –
on the trail of the Hound

A hound it was, an enormous coal-black hound, but not such a hound as mortal eyes have ever seen. Fire burst from its open mouth, its eyes glowed with a smouldering glare, its muzzle and hackles and dewlap were outlined in flickering flame. Never in the delirious dream of a disordered brain could anything more savage, more appalling, more hellish, be conceived than that dark form and savage face which broke upon us out of the wall of fog.

The Hound of the Baskervilles

On one of the evenings Arthur and Louise spent together when they were newly married, or perhaps earlier, when the two families were gathered round the fire getting to know each other, and young Innes no doubt eager to learn about the turbulent history of the Welsh borders, it is easy to imagine that Louise would have told the story of the legend of the Hound of the Vaughans, which was so well known in her native country on the borders of England and Wales. She might also have produced her copy of *Malvern Chase* for Arthur to see. The book had been published in 1881, and was enjoying great acclaim, having run to several editions. (It is now quite difficult to obtain.) No book could have described better the romance of the Hawkins' part of the world: the castles of Skenfrith, Grosmont and the White Castle, the abbeys of Llanthony, Abbey Dore and Tintern, the fortified manor houses of Pontrilas, Treago, Hergest, Kenchurch and, further west, Tretower – magical and historic names. And in it the legend of Vaughan and the Hound is recounted in detail. No doubt Arthur kept it well and truly in his mind, to be used at a later date.

Malvern Chase was written by W.S. Symonds, the Rector of Pendock. He was one of that breed of clergymen to whom we owe much, for their love and knowledge of the countryside, their classical learning and their extensive and diligent research into history. They had time for all this because usually they would have only one parish, and often a wife to oversee the smooth running of domestic affairs. Such clergymen would have had an excellent education as well as their theological learning, for they were very often the younger sons of noble families.

Malvern Chase was hailed as a well-researched and accurate account of the Wars of the Roses, an era which, of all times in English history, could be said to be the most confusing. Among the historical facts Symonds weaves a love affair of hope and despair tempered with gripping action and marvellous descriptions of the countryside, with minute attention to flora and fauna. Most intriguing of all is the way he brings the character of Master Vaughan of Hergest into the picture, together with the dreaded Black Hound.

Thomas Vaughan of Hergest is the uncle and ward of the book's heroine. A Lancastrian (here Symonds makes a mistake, for he was in fact a Yorkist), he is nevertheless a friend of the hero's parents, the Yorkist de Brutes of Birtsmorton Court, in Malvern Chase. The first mention of the Hound in the book comes when the hero, Hildebrand,

Birtsmorton Court in 1880

after a skirmish in the forest, has to stay the night at Hergest Court, near Kington. After describing the feast and the mesmerising harp music and songs of the old bard that followed, the book tells how Hildebrand is guided to his room by Master Vaughan, who is uneasy to see that he has his dog, Vulcan, with him:

> I could not have been asleep above a quarter of an hour when I was awakened by something moving at the foot of my bed, and, starting up I saw the figure of an enormous black boar-hound with glaring eyes and a most savage expression, making as if he were about to spring on the bed. Seizing my dagger, which I had placed beneath my pillow, I immediately jumped out of bed, when the black hound moved slowly towards the door, turning round from time to time uttering the 'whimp whimp' and showing his fangs and glaring eyes. Vulcan, too, hearing this, rushed from beneath the chair, and there were the two dogs confronting each other, the black hound standing exactly opposite the doorway, ready for a spring, and with his bristles standing on end and eyes which flamed like torches.
>
> I now gave the signal 'Hie! hie!' the well known cheer to every bull-dog for a rush at the bull at the stake, and Vulcan sprang towards the door. No sooner had he reached it than he cowered down to the very floor, and creeping slowly backwards on his belly with a distressing cry, as if suffering great bodily torture, he crept close to the chair and there remained soughing. Not liking to approach such an animal, and wondering how the brute got into the room, and at the cowardice of Vulcan, I was about to shout for aid, when gradually the form of the animal faded away, and I saw nothing but the massive doorway, with its great ribs of oak.
>
> Having examined the door, I found that it was fast, and lifting the latch, I looked outside, but could see nothing, and hear nothing but the sonorous sounds of heavy sleepers. I then returned to the great chair and found the dog had cowered underneath. I spoke to him, and encouraged

him again and again, but there was no movement, and on examination I found he was stone dead! I was more than startled and felt that peculiar awe which unnerves the boldest heart and pales the cheek of the bravest who has to face an apparition.

Later in the book there is a description of the Battle of Mortimer's Cross on the field of which our hero is knighted Sir Hildebrand de Brute by Duke Edward – he is still only 21. Afterwards he visits Hergest again and one of the old gardeners there tells him that he was lucky to have slept in 'the haunted room of the Black Hound' and come out alive.

References to the Hound continue throughout the book. In due course Hildebrand, still searching for his beloved Rosamond, learns that the Welsh chief Master Vaughan was wounded at the Battle of Edgecote. People had seen the shadow of a Black Hound in the forests of Hergest, a sure sign of the impending decease of the head of the family, and a few weeks later he hears that a wounded gentleman has been asking for him, and wanting to know how far it is to Birtsmorton Court. He finds it is indeed Vaughan, dying of his dreadful wounds. Vaughan is by now in a high fever, but able to tell him that he has taken Rosamond to France to place her in the safety of a convent. That night Vaughan dies of the fever.

I sat by him all that night, the fever again rose to its full height, and before midnight his spirit passed away as he was talking and gesticulating to an imaginary hound, which nothing would induce him to believe was not endeavouring to jump up on the couch. It was a sad spectacle next morning as the corpse of this gallant gentleman lay distorted, and the morning sun burst full upon it, another victim of these accursed wars ... I did all that was left to be done for the body of Rosamond's uncle and he was laid to rest in the church of Kington ...

Perhaps it was with Louise's family tales and the story of *Malvern Chase* firmly embedded in his retentive memory that Arthur decided that his next full-length book would be something similar, though he would keep the legend of the 'Hound' in reserve, ready to use when the time was right. With two friends he organised a walking holiday in the New Forest, a three-week tour in the course of which he obtained a realistic background for the story he had in mind, to be called *The White Company*. In his self-assured way he told his friends that it would be the best book ever. But its publication was delayed for some time, as other books, *The Captain of the Pole Star and other tales*, *The Firm of Girdlestone* and *Micah Clarke*, together with the emergence of Sherlock Holmes, were beginning to put him on the literary map of London.

The White Company is set in the reign of Edward III. The hero, Alleyne, has a good education, having been brought up by the monks of Beaulieu Abbey, and he goes forth into the world seeking adventure. With two staunch friends he is involved in many battles in France, where England is gradually losing all her former possessions. The descriptions of these, and the tournaments Alleyne is involved with, are vivid. He seems to meet nearly everyone in the history of that time, including King James of Majorca and 'Pedro the Cruel'. There is much conversation in a fictional version of the language of that time, with lots of 'Forsooths' and 'I'faiths'. There are great deeds of chivalry, of course; Alleyne is knighted, which brings him up to the social level of his beloved, and he rescues her just in time to escape the veil, exactly as in the story of *Malvern Chase*. It has to be said that the latter book is far more believable, and much better constructed.

The White Company falls straight into the category of the adventure books that were now becoming popular: Rider Haggard's *King Solomon's Mines* and Robert Louis Stevenson's *Treasure Island* and *Kidnapped*. Stevenson was also delving into the weird and supernatural with *Dr. Jekyll and Mr. Hyde*. *The White Company* was not very well received, and Arthur was furious. However, he would have been pleased that, many years later, Robert Baden Powell, in *Scouting for Boys*, praised *The White Company* for its 'insight into chivalry'.

In the next few years in Portsmouth Arthur threw himself into all kinds of subjects. He was interested in everything, from the writings of Carlyle to the Library and Scientific Society. His support for the new Liberal Unionists (he was elected their Vice-Chairman) involved a lot of speaking at meetings. He confessed that it was the Irish blood in him that made him enjoy this so much; he loved debate, the more heated the better. When Arthur Balfour came down to Portsmouth, speaking against Gladstone, the meeting became hot-tempered and violent, and Arthur was embroiled in a scrap in which he was knocked down. This would not have deterred him in the least. He had had plenty of boxing at university, and his description in the *Stark Munro Letters* of his fight with Budd is written as one who knows every feint and blow.

These excursions brought Arthur into the public eye and increased his flow of patients. This was just as well, for he was still finding it difficult to place his stories, until at last he hit on the idea of his two main characters. He also decided to change the way the stories were presented to the public. Up to this time, crime stories in the popular fiction magazines of the day such as the *Strand* were always published in instalments over two or three issues, but from now on Conan Doyle's Sherlock Holmes stories were published complete in one issue. The public's response seems to have been very positive: far from feeling let down, people seemed even more keen to buy and solve the next story. It was a bold decision to make, but it worked. As for coming up with the stories themselves, reading and discussing them in the evenings with Louise, his calm and astute wife, would bring a clear perspective on the problem.

These early years in Portsmouth were very happy, as is clear from Arthur's diaries. On 28 January 1889, he wrote to his mother: 'Toodles (Touie i.e. Louise) produced this morning at 6.15 a.m. a remarkably fine specimen of the Toodles minor, who is now howling her head off in the back bedroom, and I must say I am surprised at the young woman seeing both her parents are modest sort of people! She had no luggage with her nor any possessions of any kind.' Arthur was obviously thrilled at the birth. The baby continued to thrive, and later on there are several references to her chuckling good humour. Arthur said he did not tell his mother that Louise was pregnant as he thought she might be worried. As she had herself been pregnant nine times, this seems a rather weak excuse.

Chapter 6
The beginnings of fame

'Experience', said Holmes. 'Indirectly, it may be of value, you know;
you have only to put it into words to gain the reputation of being
excellent company for the remainder of your existence.

from 'The Adventure of the Engineer's Thumb'

One day in 1889, out of the blue, Arthur Conan Doyle received an invitation from Joseph Marshall Stoddart, the proprietor of a very successful magazine in America called *Lippincott's Monthly*. As Stoddart had now joined forces with Ward Lock in Britain this looked promising, and it certainly turned out to be so. They met at the Langham Hotel in Portland Place, and one of the other writers invited was Oscar Wilde. Arthur liked him a lot – they both had Irish roots – and Wilde said he had read and enjoyed Arthur's book *Micah Clarke*.

Stoddart commissioned work from both Conan Doyle and Oscar Wilde. The work Wilde produced as a result became famous as *A Picture of Dorian Gray*. Stoddart took Arthur's work on trust, and he was paid a fee of £100 for a contribution of not less than 40,000 words; the book and serial rights would add to the work's earnings. Arthur was ecstatic. He had never been paid in advance before, and this was his most significant break-though to date. He was to make this contribution a Sherlock Holmes and Dr. Watson story, and it came out as *The Sign of Four*. Stoddart's trust in Arthur was well repaid, and the partnership of Holmes and Watson was cemented for all time.

Louise had taken baby Mary to the Isle of Wight for a short holiday with the redoubtable Granny Hawkins. The christening of the baby had been at the church of St. James at Milton, which was only a walk away from Portsea, and still quite a country area. Arthur was playing a lot of cricket, with seemingly endless energy, but at the end of the 1890 season he rushed off to Berlin to hear an eminent German scientist and bacteriologist, Professor Robert Koch, who had been working on the newly discovered treatments for cholera and tuberculosis. Arthur left for Germany at very short notice, but he did manage to get letters of introduction to the British Ambassador, and the *Times* correspondent in Berlin. Throughout his life Arthur had a knack of getting letters of introduction from the 'right people'. In this he followed in the footsteps of his mother, who traded on family connections to obtain advancement for her children. It wasn't really pushiness, for the family *were* well connected – she simply wished to remind people of the fact!

On his way to Berlin Arthur met another young doctor by the name of Malcolm Morris, a specialist at St. Mary's Hospital in London. Besides being very impressed with Morris's progressive views on public health, the conversation helped to convince Arthur that London was the place to be. When he reached Germany, he found that his letters of credential did not do the trick, and he was not admitted to the lecture. He was furious, and put it down to prejudice against the British. He did manage, however, to see a copy of the lecture and this enabled him to write a letter to the *Daily Telegraph* making it clear that he had grave doubts about the Professor's methods. The main consequence of the journey was to increase Arthur's determination to move to London. But before doing so, he wanted to pursue another new enthusiasm which had recently taken hold. He decided to go to Vienna and study eye surgery (he had done some work at the Portsmouth Eye Hospital). Then, upon his move to London he would be well equipped to set up in a new field: optometry.

He wanted Louise to go with him to Austria, so arrangements were made to leave baby Mary with Granny Hawkins and the wonderful loyal old maidservant, Mrs. Bishop. The baby was not yet a year old, so it must have been a wrench for Louise to leave her. Arthur was writing stories and articles all the time now, and even in Vienna he made the most of the periods between lectures.

A very important link was made at this time. Arthur's literary agent, Alexander Watt, had sent some of Arthur's short stories to Herbert Green Hough Smith, the editor of the *Strand Magazine*, which was

concentrating on higher grade stories than those published by its rivals. The magazine was owned by the powerful George Newnes, and this alliance would last all of Arthur's writing life, including the publication of *The Hound of the Baskervilles.*

In Vienna Arthur and Louise at first stayed at the expensive Hotel Kummer, but they soon moved to a much cheaper pension. It was warm and comfortable, though, and only a short walk from his lectures; and they found their evenings full of entertainment, dancing and music. But this did not last very long. There were worries at home. Arthur's mother appears to have been in debt again and was borrowing money from Dr. Waller; and Arthur's sister Connie had fallen in love with an 'unsuitable' man in Portugal, where she and her sister Lottie were travelling. As head of the family, Arthur ordered Lottie to come home at once, and bring Connie! So the stay in Vienna was curtailed; but Arthur was not too concerned about it, for in truth his German had not been advanced enough to understand specialised lectures in eye surgery. At least he bought Professor Landholl's book, *The Refraction and Acceleration of the Eye and their Anomalies,* and it would stand him in good stead to say he had studied with such an eminent professor.

Back in Portsmouth there were many farewells to be said, for Arthur and Louise had been very popular there. They also had to find a family to take Innes, who was at that time living with them again whilst doing his 'cramming' course at Portsmouth Grammar School. In due course the Doyles moved to South Norwood, a good choice. There was easy access to London on the train, and Norwood was now turning from 'real country' into leafy suburb. It must have been hard to imagine that only fifty years before, Surtees had described Mr. Jorrocks hacking down there from London for a good day's hunting. There were still quite grand houses there with spacious gardens. The one Arthur and Louise occupied seems to have been a new house, perhaps in what had been the garden of another mansion. In an article in the *Strand Magazine* of 1892, 'Interview with Celebrities' (the term was in use even then!), 12 Tennison Road is described as 'A prettily built and modest looking red brick residence'. It was surrounded by an old stone wall, which gave the garden charm, and an area known as 'the tennis court' (presumably reflecting its previous use).

On the horizon to the north was the Crystal Palace, and the hills of Surrey, culminating in the glorious North Downs, lay to the south. The view was spectacular; on a clear day one could see right across the Weald of Kent. Perhaps the Downs reminded Louise of the Welsh hills. Arthur was now longing to explore the place; but first he arranged to rent two rooms at 25, Montague Place, which was behind the British Museum, with the intention of setting himself up as an ophthalmic surgeon, as he described himself. Of course, the location was also handy for the British Museum, where he could research his books. His story *A Scandal in Bohemia* was submitted from here, one of the first of the complete thrillers that became so popular. It is also the tale in which Sherlock Holmes almost – but not quite – falls in love. As it has a European theme, it is quite likely that Arthur started writing it in Vienna. After the rush of acceptances of the Sherlock Holmes stories Arthur took the plunge, gave up his consulting rooms and decided to make his living and his name as a writer.

Arthur was delighted with Surrey, and now that he had given up medical practice in London, he wanted to explore the countryside, 'dressed as he liked' rather than being bound up in formal city clothes. To this end he invested in one of the new machines now becoming all the rage: the tandem. Compared to today's streamlined affairs they were rugged and heavy, designed so that the rider could sit upright in a dignified fashion. They were very strong, and with the double power provided by two people they could skim along and cover the miles, and cope with the hills in an amazingly competent fashion. Arthur noted that a 15-mile run was easy. They would pause at an inn somewhere, take a midday break and return by early afternoon. They must both have become very fit, and to suggest, as some biographers have done, that Louise was always 'delicate' is not borne out by the evidence. Only once, at the beginning of 1892, is it recorded that Louise came back by train, and that day the trip would have been 100 miles! She may have had the instinct that she was ready to conceive again and was taking care; her son was born less than twelve months later.

This was the time when the young couple were closest. Not only did they spend most of their days together; in the evenings they would plot

Arthur and Touie on their tandem tricycle

out the new Sherlock Holmes stories which were now being eagerly accepted. At this time Arthur noted that he often had a bet with Louise that she would not guess the identity of the 'real' criminal in some of his plots, but that – with her feminine intuition and her amazingly cool thinking – she always did. He treated her collaboration with the greatest respect. Her inspiration and ideas were a great help to him and these stories were an immediate success. They were to ensure Arthur's popularity for all time and no future series ever came up to their level. *He had made the great break-through with the inspiration of Louise at his side.*

The Speckled Band is probably the best known and most intriguing of

all the Sherlock Holmes short stories, and was later made into a popular West End play. It is set in Surrey, not far from Leatherhead, and therefore not far from Norwood, where Louise and Arthur lived, and in the area they explored on their tandem. Was the idea of the snake wound round the head of the victim suggested by the heraldic crest of the Vaughans – a boy's head with a snake wrapped round his neck?

On the domestic front, Arthur wrote to his mother that Mary, now two and a half, was a wonderful mimic and the greatest fun. In November 1892 Arthur's son was born, and named Arthur Alleyne Kingsley Conan Doyle – to be called Kingsley. The baby was strong and healthy, and grew up to be good-looking and clever. His sister Mary adored him, and the family seemed complete. Having returned from Portugal, Arthur's sister Connie

Above: the Vaughan coat of arms
Below: Touie with young Mary and Kingsley

was now doing some typing for him, and had fallen in love with a promising young writer, E.W. Hornung. His stories of the gentleman burglar Raffles, to be published as *The Amateur Cracksman*, were to strike gold with the reading public. Arthur liked 'young Willie' Hornung very much, and a few months later, in 1893, Connie married him.

With the success of the Sherlock Holmes stories, Arthur could refurbish the house, buy a fur coat for Touie and also invest some money. In July 1893 he accepted an offer to lecture for an up and coming magazine, *The Young Man* – not obviously on his wavelength as it was a Christian-sponsored paper and the editor was a Methodist. It was promoting its Lucerne gathering with a special offer of nine days' inclusive holiday, including travelling expenses, for £8. Arthur was pleased to find that this opportunity led to his meeting some distinguished people, including Henry Lunn, who with his brother was set up the famous travel firm Lunns Tours, and Benjamin Waugh, who founded the National Society for the Prevention of Cruelty to Children in 1884.

Arthur insisted that Louise should accompany him, even though Kingsley was barely eight months old, so again the babies were left with the redoubtable Granny Hawkins. After this journey to Switzerland, having walked long distances with Arthur, each of his walking companions in turn laid claim to the idea that Arthur should plan Sherlock Holmes' death in the Reichenbach Falls. (Arthur had told everybody that he wanted to get rid of Holmes.) Louise accompanied the men on these walks, some of them very tough going, and was referred to as 'that plucky little wife of Arthur Conan Doyle'.

In October 1893 Arthur's father died. The death had been expected, but the family who had known the gentle person he had been before his decline must have mourned a shattered life. That Arthur did not go to the funeral perhaps shows that he had the Victorian attitude that mental illness brought shame upon a family. He certainly did not want it talked about, and discouraged discussion even within the family. However, the obituary for his father in the *Scotsman* was kindly put and described him fairly as 'a most likeable man, genial, entertaining and amusing'. It went on to say: 'He was a great reader and in consequence well-informed. His abilities and gentlemanly manner secured to him a cordial welcome wherever he went.' This carefully omits to say that he had destroyed his artistic talent and his brain through his addiction to alcohol.

Following this came far worse news. Louise, who had been struggling with a troublesome cough, was diagnosed as having tuberculosis. To quote Arthur, 'It was the great misfortune that darkened and deflected our lives.'

The Adventures of Sherlock Holmes and *Memoirs of Sherlock Holmes* were printed by Newnes, and Holmes himself had now disappeared over the Reichenbach Falls. It is said that in the City of London the clerks wore black armbands. Louise was to spend the winter in Davos, and Arthur, after his current lecture tour, would join her there. No longer would his wife be sitting at his elbow, observing, commenting and engaging with him in the planning, ideas and inspiration of his most popular stories.

In Arthur's preface to *Sherlock Holmes: the Complete Short Stories,* written in 1928, he wrote of Holmes that: 'As a witty critic remarked, "He may not have been killed when he fell over the cliff, but he was never quite the same man afterwards."' Arthur precedes this quotation against himself by saying that 'as Holmes's methods and character became familiar to the public there was naturally less element of surprise, and the later stories suffered by comparison'. To my mind, though, he must also have been aware that there were many who said that none of the Sherlock Holmes stories ever came up to the ones he wrote with Louise at his side.

Chapter 7
So much for chivalry!

It has long been an axiom of mine that the little things are infinitely the most important.

Sherlock Holmes, from 'A Case of Identity'

After the diagnosis Louise lived on for another thirteen years, at least in part due to the wonderful care Arthur insisted she received, mostly in Switzerland. He did not curtail his heavy schedule of lecture tours but he always went back to Louise when he could. His description of their movements to a friend are typically humorous. When they travel, he says, they are like a migratory tribe, 'a nurse, a maid, all sorts of retainers, all sorts of scouts, sisters, sisters-in-law leave or re-join at uncertain intervals, add to this the children and governess and one gets some idea!'

In 1894 he went on a hectic three-month lecture tour in America, on which he was accompanied by Innes – good education for the young officer. In the autumn of 1895 Arthur and Louise set off for a holiday in Egypt. Writing from the Mena House Hotel in Cairo, Arthur noted: 'Touie loves dancing with the Military!' Gillian Hodges of Aymestrey has kindly shown me a beautifully written diary kept by her aunt, Miss Ethel Ward of Yatton Court. In it Ethel, then also in Cairo, writes: 'Mrs Conan Doyle has just come a cropper against a tree, and smashed her bicycle!' – which shows that Louise must still have been strong and active at that time. The Doyles went on a Nile cruise (a 'Cooks' new Steamboat Services Offer) and Arthur noted that Louise was doing well. Then fighting broke out between the British and the Dervishes, and Arthur contacted the *Westminster Gazette* offering his services as a war correspondent. In this capacity he went to the war zone at Wadi Halfa and heard talk of a rising young officer called Kitchener.

In 1896 he came back to England to buy a beautiful plot of land at Hindhead in Surrey. Touie returned with him, but once the deal was done she went back to Switzerland, taking the children with her.

The house at Hindhead was taking a long time in the planning and building, so Arthur rented a comfortable house at Grayswood Beeches near Haslemere. This was a great success. Mary, now nearly seven, and Kingsley a lively four-year-old, had the run of the place and kept lots of pets, rabbits and chickens – it was a child's paradise. Granny Hawkins joined them with Louise, who was holding her own. Arthur was now thinking of putting *Sherlock Holmes* on as a stage play.

At the end of October 1897 they moved into the Hindhead house, 'Undershaw'. Covering 4 acres of the finest upland country of Surrey, it included a lodge, stables and a coach house, a tennis court, wine cellars, servants' quarters and a power plant to provide electricity for the whole establishment. There were eleven bedrooms and plenty of bathrooms. Louise had a Broadwood piano, and Arthur bought her a Landau. For himself he acquired a new hunter whom he named 'The Brigadier' (after his recent book), a 'useful' type of horse, well up to carrying Arthur's weight, which was now over 15 stone. He took up hunting, and when the 'season' was over, it was the time of year for cricket, at which he excelled. He was now playing the part of a country squire. He wrote hunting poems and hunting songs, gave lectures, and paid for it all from the proceeds of the Sherlock Holmes stories.

All would have been well, but sadly a disruptive force now entered their lives in the form of a young woman called Jean Leckie. The person who observed this with increasing disquiet was Arthur's brother Innes. In the two years since Undershaw had been the Conan Doyle family's home, Innes had stayed there whenever he liked, treating it as his home. Arthur bought an extra hunter for him, and as a young officer he had enjoyed the social life to the full besides being devoted to his little niece and nephew.

At the end of 1898 Arthur hosted a costume ball for 200 guests – not at his house but at the Beacon Hotel. There was a great variety of costumes; Arthur himself went dressed as a Viking, and his daughter Mary was allowed to attend dressed as a 'forget-me-not'. In his diary Innes said they danced until 5 am! By this time in his life Innes had achieved his dream and had been commissioned in the Royal Artillery. He was posted to India in 1899 and arrived in Bombay on 19 May. In the time-honoured way, his sister Lottie, who was of marriageable age, was sent out to join Innes and keep house for him, in the hope that she would meet someone who would be a suitable match. In the event, on the ship on the way out to India Lottie met the Oldham family, who were travelling to India to see their son Captain Leslie William Piers Oldham of the Royal Engineers, recently back from the famous Relief of Chitral in 1895, where he was mentioned in dispatches. One thing led to another, Lottie married Captain Oldham, and it was a very happy marriage. They had a daughter named Claire.

While Innes was in India he decided to write to Arthur about Jean Leckie. While staying at Undershaw before his posting, he had seen that Jean was a very frequent guest. It must have been very hard for Louise to bear the company of this young woman of 22, who rode well, was perfectly and expensively dressed, and musically trained as a solo singer. Most of the family remarked that she liked to 'play the gallery' and be the centre of attention.

At this time Innes himself had been hoping to marry, but the girl he was in love with, Dora Hamilton, had married someone else, so perhaps he was feeling a bit of an expert on affairs of the heart. At Undershaw, he had certainly been able to see the drama being played out in front of his eyes, for whilst out hunting he had broken his collarbone in a fall, and this grounded him. Housebound for a few days, he would have had the chance to have long talks with Louise and, although she never voiced her unhappiness to him, he was well able to sense it. Jean Leckie was now a frequent visitor; Arthur was having his portrait painted (his own idea) and Jean in her forward way had asked for the famous painter's autograph (the painter was Sidney Paget, who at the time was producing illustrations for Arthur's stories). By any standards it was cruel of Arthur to invite this volatile young woman to his house so often. Louise was a wonderful manager and had plenty of servants to help, but it must have been quite tiring ensuring that everything ran smoothly, and she was shortly to lose Lottie, who had been a staunch helper, who was to accompany Innes to India.

Arthur's bland reply to Innes sidestepped the issue. There is no doubt at all that he was bowled over by Jean Leckie from the first;

but he maintained that it was always a platonic relationship. Certainly any scandal would have ruined him. Jean's parents were very wealthy and early on, in breathtakingly bad taste, they gave Arthur a gift of a diamond and pearl pin stud, as though he was already a son-in-law!

Innes as a cadet at Woolwich (photograph courtesy of Mrs. Georgina Doyle)

Arthur's letter to Innes was very carefully worded:

> My last letter about my private affairs must have surprised
> you rather. You need not fear that any harm will arise from
> it, or that any pain will be given to Touie. She is as dear
> to me as ever, but as I said, there is a large side of my life
> which was unoccupied, but is no longer so. It will all fit in
> very well and nobody the worse off, and two of us be very
> much better. I shall see to it very carefully that no harm
> comes to anyone. I say all this lest you, at a distance, might
> fear that we were drifting towards trouble!

This strange letter could be interpreted in several ways. For Arthur
to say that no pain would be given to Touie seems self-deluding; she
had been hurt already. By the time Innes returned from his foreign
service in India and China almost three years had passed and the affair
had advanced into the now well-known extraordinary 'grand opera'.
The family felt that Arthur was almost besotted, and their dislike of
Jean was increasing. In a census of 1901 we see that Arthur Conan
Doyle, a physician, was living at Ashdown Forest Hotel, Forest Row,
Sussex. Also resident there were Mary J. Doyle, aged 63, born Lismore,
Ireland, and Jean E. Leckie, aged 27, born Blackheath. It appears from
this that Arthur's mother had not only accepted the situation between
her son and Jean Leckie but was staying at the same hotel to give the
situation respectability. So much for chivalry! Arthur's mother does not
shine in this episode, or later.

An old friend of Louise remarked that she thought that Louise was
well aware of the situation, but, well aware too of her fragile health, she
had accepted it as inevitable. Only once did Arthur ever slip up socially
so that he was 'seen' with Jean, and that was one day at the M.C.C.
when they were together and ran straight into sister Connie and Willie
Hornung. Connie was furious, and it caused quite a rift for some time
between her and her brother. Jean Leckie was young (then only 27),
self-assured (a trained singer), and determined that one day she would
marry this famous character. She encouraged him completely in his
growing belief in spiritualism and séances, which eventually made him
a laughing stock.

Despite all this intrigue, Arthur continued to be full of enthusiasm for other projects. He had wanted to enlist for the Boer War but was too old. Never defeated, he helped John Langman to set up volunteers for a medical team. By 1900 he was at Bloemfontein and sent a descriptive piece about converting the cricket pavilion there into a hospital. By June he was with the South African Field Force at the Langman Hospital. His reports touched the nation. They were so alive and descriptive that later on he was commissioned to write the history of the Boer War for the Government.

On the voyage home he met an ambitious young journalist called Fletcher Robinson, who realised at once the advantage that close friendship with this famous author could give. Robinson told Arthur that he lived on Dartmoor, and invited him to stay. Robinson's father was an influential man, an added attraction for Arthur. Arthur told Robinson of his plans to 'bring Sherlock Holmes back to life' (having at last realised what a money-spinner Holmes was). The legend of the Hound of the Vaughans was still in Arthur's head, but he had never found the exact background he wanted. But suddenly, staying on Dartmoor, Arthur saw what a perfect setting it would make. In March 1901 he wrote to his mother that he and Fletcher Robinson were going to do a small book together, to be called *The Hound of the Baskervilles* – a real creeper! The first instalment was published in the *Strand Magazine* in August 1901.

A few years ago Professor Christopher Frayling made a careful film on the writing of 'The Hound', in which he noted that Arthur altered the dedication in several succeeding editions of the book, each time subtly diminishing Fletcher Robinson's role in the creation of *The Hound of the Baskervilles*. In the first printing Arthur said he owed 'the inception' and 'the general plot and the local details' (i.e. Dartmoor) to Fletcher Robinson. But the second printing told a different story. He gave no more than a casual 'thank you' to Fletcher Robinson for a 'chance remark', and stated very deliberately 'Every word is my own'. When Fletcher Robinson gave a copy of the book to his coachman, who happened to have the name Baskerville, it was inscribed by Robinson but not signed by Arthur, and simply said 'Thank you for letting the name be used.' One senses a certain severing in the friendship with Robinson. Professor Frayling also mentioned that the editor of the

Strand had said to a friend that the story was in fact based on a Welsh legend.

Although it is believed that Arthur gave his word to a member of the Baskerville family of Herefordshire that he would make it clear they were not connected with his story, he did *not* do so clearly at any time. Nor did he give a written disclaimer. Consequently, almost immediately after the book was published, the rumours and arguments started. Writers in magazines, journalists and freelance authors, all determined to make their name, came up to Herefordshire and the Borders, eager to interview any member of the Baskerville family they could find.

As we all know, the book remains a winner. But the end of the story of Arthur and Louise must be told. She came to London for the Coronation: 'Touie is on good form and I have got a window for her at Morleys Hotel.' In October 1902 he was knighted, and Louise was present for a wonderful family party afterwards. At this time he was busy writing *The Return of Sherlock Holmes*. He was also made Deputy-Lieutenant of Surrey, but his attempts to be elected an M.P. never bore fruit. He continued to be showered with awards. In 1905 he was offered an LLD by Edinburgh University, and lecturing at Cambridge University on 22 May he noted, 'I made the most successful speech of my life' in front of the Prince of Wales and four hundred medics.

At home, though, things were not so good. He took Louise to yet another consultant as she was losing weight rapidly, and in June 1906 he wrote to Innes, 'Poor Touie delirious, she is painless in body, and easy in mind – taking it all with her usual sweet and gentle equanimity.' Finally, on July 4th, a telegram was sent: 'She passed in peace.' Louise's sister Emily ('Nem') was at her bedside along with Arthur, Mary who was 17 and Kingsley, who was 15 and soon to start at Eton. 'My father sat by the bedside,' Mary remembered 'the tears coursing down his rugged face, her small white hand enfolded in his huge grasp.' Later, Arthur wrote to his mother, 'I tried to give her every attention, every comfort she could want; did I succeed? God knows I hope so.' Thus ended this marriage of love and companionship that had been such a springboard for Arthur's talents, and the financial foundation of his career.

The locket Arthur gave Louise after their marriage
(photographs courtesy of Mrs. Georgina Doyle)

Chapter 8
After Louise

'Circumstantial evidence is a very tricky thing', answered Holmes thoughtfully. 'It may seem to point very straight to one thing, but if you shift your point of view a little, you may find it pointing in an equally uncompromising manner to something entirely different.'

The Boscombe Valley Mystery

It was necessary for Arthur and his sister-in-law 'Nem' to sign the Declarations so that Nem could inherit her late sister's properties, set up so carefully in old Jeremiah's will. For this they would not have had to travel in person to Monmouth or Gloucester – it could all be done through solicitors, and we see from the copies of the documents in Powys Archives and Gloucester Records that this was probably the case.

In September 1906 Arthur wrote to his mother that he was lecturing on the 'Brigadier' stories with great success and had 'carried Edinburgh by storm'. 'You would have been pleased to see your three "boys" (on stage by request!) – Kingsley, Innes and me!' Three generations whose lives had been helped and whose loyalty had been bound by the influence and loving care Louise had given each one.

Arthur prided himself on his care for his family. It worried him when he had no money, and there is no doubt that as soon as he was successful, he did his duty by them all. There is however a sad debit side. It was a flaw in his character that he treated Louise's children so callously after her death. They were at a vulnerable age. Mary was seventeen, a thoughtful, intelligent and observant girl with classical good looks and a great talent for music. Kingsley was quiet and a deep thinker, had adored his mother, and respected his father highly. Both had been a great joy to Arthur – he wrote in his memoirs, during the time Louise was so ill that: 'Mary and Kingsley were passing through the various sweet phases of human development, and brought great happiness into our lives' – but after he remarried they received neither love nor guidance from him, at a time when they needed his support badly.

It was predictable that at Mary's age there would have been feminine rivalry with her stepmother, but Arthur handed over the reins to Jean completely and overlooked petty spites which exacerbated the situation. Mary once described her father as a 'huge, kindly person, only occasionally seen and rather awe-inspiring'. At the age of ten she had composed an interesting short story about opening her umbrella and being transported to 'Elysian Fields' which had delighted Arthur so much that he had had it published by Constable of Edinburgh, complete with spelling mistakes.

Before Louise died she had told her daughter gently not to be shocked or surprised if her father should marry again. This was her wise way of preparing the teenage girl, and forestalling any jealousy she might feel.

Crowborough as it was when Arthur Conan Doyle went to live at nearby Windlesham with his second wife, Jean Leckie

At the time the marriage took place, Kingsley was beginning his first year at Eton, and looking forward to a completely new set of challenges and surroundings. Their old family friend, Julia Pocock, now finding some acclaim as an artist, was a shoulder to lean on in the holidays. She had been a good support to their mother, and gave them a link with the past. The situation did not improve and at Christmas 1908, Kingsley was allowed home, but Mary had to spend the holiday on her own in Dresden, where she was studying music. There was a new baby at Windlesham in March, so there was no going home for Kingsley in the Easter holidays, but Mary wanted him to go to Dresden and stay with her. Arrangements were made, but when Mary asked for some extra money so that she and Kingsley could go to Berlin and see an opera she was studying, her father sent her a cheque for £10, but then put her in a horrible dilemma by saying that she would have to choose between having the money or having Kingsley to stay as he could not afford both. Mary eventually persuaded him, but it was a petty thing to do, and nonsensical, as Arthur was a very rich man by now.

The estrangement went on. Kingsley wrote to his father at one stage apologising for upsetting him and asking what he had done wrong. Arthur softened up with the arrival of a new son, and things calmed down for a time. But the next move on Jean's part was cruelty itself. Mary had returned to Germany hoping to take a course in voice composition with Professor Albert Fuchs of the Dresden Royal Conservatory. Once there, she was terribly upset to receive a letter from her father saying that she was not up to it; her singing was 'flat' and she did not have a good enough ear. Presumably Jean was behind this. The fact that Mary had been accepted as a pupil by Professor Fuchs shows that she had outstanding talent. She was allowed to continue her music course, but her confidence and ambition had been taken away. As the singer of the family her stepmother had no intention of allowing a young rival to take the limelight.

Immersed in his writings and public meetings, the self-centred Arthur hardly noticed what was happening. He was becoming more and more like 'Mr. Toad of Toad Hall'. Anything new that took his or Jean's fancy – cars, for instance – had to be bought, all indulgences being made possible by the financial return from his writing and lecturing, founded, of course, on Sherlock Holmes.

Retribution, if one believes in such a thing, came very swiftly for the lack of care that Arthur had shown to Louise's children. Both his sons by Jean were spoilt from the moment they were born. The eldest, Denis Percy Stewart Conan Doyle, was born on 17 March 1909 (and died in 1955), and his younger brother, Adrian Malcolm (1910-1970), was born only a year and nine months later. They were sent to the Beacon Prep School at Crowborough and there was trouble right from the start. Once or twice they narrowly escaped being expelled and were only allowed to stay because of Arthur's influence (and probably his money). Denis did not go to Eton but became a fortnightly boarder at Tonbridge, very near his home, but something must have gone wrong there, for he went on to Berrow near Eastbourne after only a year. Soon after this he was handed over to a private tutor, who, it is said, eventually gave up on him. Adrian had much the same record. Arthur seemed unable to resist them. They demanded cars and motorcycles and got them, and then entered the social whirl, frequenting the Florida and Blue Lagoon clubs among others. There were plenty of girls and scandals around their London flat life. To make matters worse, when their aunt Connie died she left them £500, which was then a tidy sum, a nice little bonus to be spent swiftly on all the wrong things. Arthur even told Adrian, who was by now going to seed very quickly, that he and Jean did not want him to spend time with them in their lovely cottage in the New Forest, Bignall Wood.

There were motoring offences as well as frequent trouble with the police. Arthur was trying to introduce Adrian to spiritualism, but he must have chided himself for not insisting they both go to Eton, where they would have had discipline – assuming, of course, that Eton would have accepted them. On one occasion Arthur had a massive heart attack while remonstrating with Denis about his chosen girlfriend. He had just lent Adrian £500 to buy a Frazer-Nash which both sons raced in the Cambridge Speed Trials in March 1931. When Denis left his course at Cambridge, his college had no record of his having done any work at all. It is a sorry end to Arthur's family life. Both boys and their sister accompanied their father on his African tour in 1929, but how many times must he have questioned himself about his responsibility for their upbringing? His daughter 'Billie' was the only member of Jean's family who gave no trouble. Christened Lena Jean Annette and born in 1912, she died in 1997. She saw herself as a 'tomboy' until her teens, but at Granville House School in Eastbourne and then her aunt Ida's school, she presented no problems. She made a career in the Women's Royal Air Force, and by the time of her retirement she had attained the highest rank in the WRAF, Air Commandant. She made a late marriage with Air Vice Marshal Sir Geoffrey Bromet, whom she married on 11 June 1965, at St. Clement Dane's Church in the Strand. She was kind to her half-sister Mary, and saw to it that, when the time came, Mary was taken care of in a good retirement home.

Tribute to Kingsley

In contrast with the sons born of his second marriage, no man could have been more blessed than Arthur with the first son born to him on 15 November 1892. He was named Arthur Alleyne Kingsley – Arthur, of course, after his father, Alleyne after the hero of *The White Company*, and Kingsley after a family friend, Kingsley Milbourne. The little boy was strong and healthy, and possessed of very good looks and a quick intellect. Perhaps the most precious trait of all was the equable and sweet temperament he had inherited from his mother.

He and his sister were with their mother in Switzerland for two winters, and as he learned to speak, his father, delighted with his observations, noted down some of his sayings: 'He nearly always repeats himself – 'He did got down – he did' and after he had taken him to Church 'Why doesn't that man put his shirt inside his trousers?' Looking at me after I had shaved he said 'When did you get that fur?!' Later on he was a perfect mimic, particularly of his piano teacher and his grandmother. He and his sister Mary were devoted to one another. At Grayshott Beeches, the house in Haslemere, they were allowed a good deal of freedom and their father encouraged this, but always insisted that they were on time for meals, duly scrubbed and tidy.

When he was old enough Kingsley went to Sandroyd Prep. School, not far away. He immediately showed great intelligence, and was also quite an 'all-rounder' at sport, particularly cricket, which pleased his father. He went to Eton in November 1906, a month after his mother died. The first day at school is a very important day for any boy, but it was not his father who took him there (he was too busy with lectures), but his devoted and kindly uncle Innes. It is from now on, and particularly after Arthur's marriage to Jean Leckie, that we see his father treating Kingsley with increasing coolness. He worked hard and did extremely well at Eton. He left in 1910 and the summing up of his time there by his house tutor, Mr. Vaughan, is exemplary: 'In his character he has a delightful combination of strength and gentleness, independence

and loyalty; and anyone who won his friendship never lost it.' No wonder his sister Mary adored him and relied on him as if he were an older brother, especially now with the spiteful restrictions that were being put on their lives by their stepmother.

Kingsley had decided at school that he wanted to become a doctor, but before he began his training he was to have a year in Lausanne. He would then start as a medical student at St. Mary's Hospital, London. Their old family friend 'Juey', Julia Pocock, had purchased a house in London, and luckily Kingsley and Mary were able to live with her, for both of them were very unwelcome in Arthur's home with his new wife at Windlesham. It is shocking that Kingsley was accused of some minor lack of manners towards Jean by Arthur, and that at one stage he wrote to his father asking what he had done wrong.

Above: A rare moment of recognition: the watch Arthur gave to Kingsley for his 21st birthday
Below: Kingsley at Medical College (both photos courtesy of Mrs. Georgina Doyle)

By the outbreak of war, although now starting his medical career, Kingsley felt that he would serve his country better by joining the Armed Forces. He joined the 1st Battalion, Hampshire Regiment on 7 April 1915, and was commissioned as Temporary Lieutenant in February 1916. Just before the Battle of the Somme Arthur was briefly out at the Front to report on the progress of the war for the Allies and to meet General Haig, and met Kingsley out there. He only wrote that he found his son 'with his usual jolly grin upon his weather-stained features'. Shortly afterwards Kingsley was wounded in the neck, but he recovered and rejoined his unit two months later.

In April 1917 his Commanding Officer noted the care that Kingsley took over his men. On May 3rd '... the enemy had got the range of a railway arch over our H.Q., and a previous unit had used the arch as a Regimental Aid Post – some twenty poor fellows lay there only a few yards away who had made the great sacrifice. The *heat* there was almost tropical. *Something had to be done* – it was one of those jobs that was nobody's job – Kingsley Conan Doyle did it.' Finally he said: 'His enthusiasm was literally infectious, his loyalty to his superiors, his sympathy with his men, his intense patriotism and his keen sense of duty, made him a natural soldier.'

He was released early in 1918 as the War Office felt it would be better for him to complete his medical training, doctors being so badly needed. But the Spanish 'flu then raging took Kingsley. He had probably been weakened by his time in the trenches, and although he was only 26 his body could not take it. Mary, his sister, arranged for him to be buried next to his mother at Grayshott on 1st November. She must have had a terrible time at his funeral.

Arthur, it was noted, remained calm and self-controlled. He had so many times tried to make his son believe in spiritualism, but Kingsley had never veered from his Christian beliefs. Perhaps, although Kingsley had not encouraged a rift with his father over this subject, his steady refusal to give way had irritated Arthur. And when it came to Arthur's relationship with Jean, and the hurt he had inflicted on Louise, something in his son's clear gaze perhaps troubled him and made him question his own integrity. Arthur wrote no obituary for his son, and nor did he write a monograph he had promised.

But perhaps Arthur was more moved than he cared to admit. In the story called 'His Last Bow', which is set just before the Great War, Sherlock Holmes says: 'Good old Watson! you are the one fixed point in a changing age. There's an East wind coming, such a wind as never blew on England yet. It will be cold and bitter and a good many of us may wither in its blast. But it's God's own wind none the less, and a cleaner, better, stronger land will lie in the sunshine when the storm has cleared.' Arthur's own experience of that icy wind was bitter indeed. Not only was there the loss of Kingsley; Innes too, by now a Brigadier General, died in 1918, from pneumonia after being badly wounded. These events, not so many years after the loss of Louise as well, made Arthur severely depressed and brought to an end the wonderful exuberance he had always had, and his way of taking up challenge after challenge with the complete self-belief that had always been the hallmark of the heroes of his books.

Towards the End

There had been so many instances of 'set up' séances, and false 'mediums' that it is amazing Arthur did not give up his belief in spiritualism. It is estimated that he gave thousands of pounds in support of the spiritualist movement; perhaps he felt that he had given so much money to the cause that he could not have faced becoming a laughing stock if he had given up on it. After he died, his wife Jean organised a huge memorial service in the Albert Hall, and put the word round to over 6,000 people who were eager to attend that he would undoubtedly appear to speak to them from the other side. There was a clairvoyant present, a Miss Estelle Robert, who suddenly announced in the silence 'He is here'. She walked across to Jean and had a whispered conversation. Later she said, 'He gave me a personal message for Lady Doyle – but I must not repeat it – he was wearing evening dress and I saw him distinctly.'

What a cruel let down! My father remarked that not only those present but hundreds of thousands of people still grieving for their shocking losses in the 1914-18 War must have had even those slender hopes shattered. Hugh Walpole noted in his diary 'Conan Doyle dead. A brave, simple childish man. How hard he tried to make me a spiritualist!'

Finis

The interfamily financial and legal disputes resulting from Arthur's death went on and on, and after Denis died, Adrian and his sister-in-law were locked in interminable battles. Ken McCormick, Editor-in-

Chief of Arthur's prestigious American publishers, Doubleday, is heard to have remarked 'I shudder at the thought of getting involved in this, because everybody in the family is so unbelievably unpleasant.'

Not that this is the impression given by subsequent biographies of Arthur Conan Doyle. Nor is the importance to Arthur of his first marriage made clear – the efforts of his second wife, Lady Conan Doyle, to minimise what it meant to him and his career made sure of that. There have been many biographies written about Arthur Conan Doyle, but when John Dickson Carr's came out it sent shockwaves through all those who had known Arthur throughout his first marriage and were aware of the love and inspiration Louise had brought to him. The comments in this book were at best negative and at worst antagonistic. To support his mother, Adrian Doyle had fed in many ideas which were completely untrue. Hurt and horrified at this injustice to her mother, Mary wrote to the *Daily Telegraph* and her letter was printed on 19 March 1949 (and published afterwards in America):

```
    Sir,
                Louise Conan Doyle

    I would like to draw attention to the way
in which my mother's character is portrayed
in the recent biography of my father by Mr
John Dickson Carr. She was certainly not the
negative, colourless and rather insipid person
he depicts her as being. It might appear from
the foreword to the book that Mr Dickson Carr
had consulted me about my mother, and the
'Undershaw' days, but this, I regret, he did
not do, although he did ask once about my
father.
    I first read the chapter dealing with my
mother when I bought a copy of the book the
other day.
    I feel one gets a very wrong impression of
Louise Conan Doyle in the biography,

                        Yours faithfully,

                        Mary Conan Doyle
```

In view of the fact that Mary must have felt so angry, hurt and affronted, this is a very restrained letter. A spinster, now elderly, standing alone, she knew that she had very little chance of being believed. Had Kingsley survived and taken his place as head of the family, things would have been very different.

One of the sad results of a book such as the biography written by John Dickson Carr is that (as it is well written and most of its content has quite detailed research), it is taken as the truth, and other writers refer to it as such. That is exactly what happened here. It is not until Andrew Lycett's book, *The man who created Sherlock Holmes*, that we get a more balanced account of Arthur's first marriage, and a little more light is shed on the mystery of Arthur, Louise and the true Hound of the Baskervilles.

Appendix 1
Sightings of the Hound of the Vaughans

'Is there any other point to which you wish to draw my attention?'
'To the curious incident of the dog in the night-time.'
'The dog did nothing in the night-time.'
'That was the curious incident,' remarked Sherlock Holmes.

Silver Blaze

In 1919, so many stories about the Black Hound were being told around Kington that my father decided to gather together a few statements from 'credible witnesses'. It has to be said that at this time the Hound was not the only subject of general rumour of this sort. There seems to have been a fascination about the mysterious appearances of strange animals. For example, Francis Kilvert's diary entry of Friday 16th August 1872 reads:

> The stories about the baboon of Maesllwych Castle grows more and more extraordinary – it is said that when visitors come to the Castle the creature descends upon their heads clambering down the balusters of the staircase. He put Baskerville [this would have been Ralph's father of Clyro Court] and Apperley to flight, routed them horse and foot, so that they clapped spurs to their horses, and galloped away in mortal fear, the baboon racing after them. He carries the cats to the top of the highest Castle Tower, and drops them into space – and it is believed that the baboon seeks an opportunity to carry the young heir to the top of the Tower and serve him in the same way.

This was of course nearly forty years before; however, it was known that the Wilkins family at Maesllwych, who were immensely

Maesllwch Castle by Joseph Murray Ince

rich through the East India Company in Bengal, had changed their family name to de Winton following the hanging of Mary Morgan, which had shown them in a bad light. The rumour was that the appearances of this baboon, spectral or otherwise, were connected with their reputation. And then, as now, stories of sightings of black panther-type cats were legion. Indeed, it is not impossible that a big cat that had been kept in captivity could have escaped to roam the countryside. The keeping of exotic animals was fashionable in Arthur's time, as described in his story 'The Brazilian Cat', in which the eponymous 'cat' is described by its murderous keeper:

> Some people call it a black puma, but really it is not a puma at all. That fellow is nearly eleven feet from tail to tip. Four years ago he was a little ball of back fluff, with two yellow eyes staring out of it. He was sold me as a new-born cub up in the wild country at the head-waters of the Rio Negro. They speared his mother to death after she had killed a dozen of them.

The following is the account given to my father by a Mrs. Gladys Owens of Hergest Court Farm, whom my father described as 'an ordinary sensible woman of good education':

MRS. GLADYS OWENS' STATEMENT

I am the Wife of Arthur Percy Owens of Hergest Court Farm, to whom I have been married seven years. I have three children.

About two years ago in the Winter time, I was sitting in the Sitting-room waiting up for my husband who had gone into Kington. My baby was sleeping in his cot near me.

It was about eleven o'clock at night. The door of the Sitting-room was ajar as the lock was broken.

I was sitting on a level with the door reading, when suddenly I heard something coming down the passage from the large oak Dining-room.

I listened, to hear what it was, as I thought it was a rat, but to my horror I could tell at once it was no rat.

I could hear what seemed like a heavy four-footed animal shuffling down the passage, and it seemed to be snuffling or snorting with its nose near the ground, and it was going from side to side of the passage. It did not come straight at all.

I was petrified with fright, but I had the presence of mind to jump up and bang the door to. I simply banged it to and held it. I could not look up the passage.

The hound, of course, came into my mind when I knew it was not a rat.

I am not of an excitable temperament, and have lived here seven years.

I know the sound of a rat.

I am absolutely certain it was the hound.

My husband has tried to alter my opinion, but the snuffling noise and the shuffling of the paws, and the peculiar noise, as if it were a heavy animal, and the breathing, were unmistakable.

This was the undoubted noise of a heavy animal shuffling along from side to side.

I was, of course, hysterical with fright when my husband returned.

Since the occurrence, I have never stayed in the house by myself.

We had no dog in the house, or other animal.

Signed Gladys Owens
Jan. 1919

Hergest Court, Kington

Mrs. Owens' statement impressed my father because of its clarity, and because Mrs. Owens told him that she had been born and bred in the country, and knew well the strange sounds of night. Perhaps, though, she was startled by a sound no one would expect to hear inside a house. A thought occurs that the vast extent of cellars under Hergest Court could have been explored by a boar badger who suddenly found himself above ground. The cry of a badger is said to be quite terrifying, and it might plausibly be mistaken for a spectral hound.

After the Owenses had left Hergest (which they did quite soon after this terrifying experience!), my father spoke to the incoming tenant, a man called John Morris, who told him that 'he didn't believe in anything like that'. Nevertheless, when *he* gave up the tenancy, John Morris spoke to Bob Jenkins, the well-known owner of the bookshop in Duke Street, Kington, and said: 'I've seen and heard things in Hergest you would never believe.' Bob repeated this in a *Hereford Times* report.

Whatever the truth of Mrs. Owens' experience might have been, my father was so impressed by her matter of fact statement that later he told my grandmother about it, and this gave her the courage to tell her own story. (My family were living in Worthing at the time, as my father had moved them from London soon after 1917 and the zeppelin raids – my brother was only a year old.) This is what my grandmother said:

```
              MRS. EMMA TURNER'S STATEMENT

I was married in 1872, and lived with my Husband
at a house near Hergest Court Farm, Kington. My
Husband and I were living there while our house
in Kington was being got ready for us. The house
at Hergest where we lived was about 1½ or 2 miles
from Kington.
   One night, at about ten o'clock, in the Winter
time (in December) my Husband and I were walking
from Kington to Hergest. We had with us a cross-
bred dog named 'Lion', which my Husband and I
usually took with us to Hergest at night for our
protection. The dog belonged to my father-in-law,
who lived at Arrow Lodge, Kington.
   We had got past the toll-gate and were getting
close to Hergest Court, when my Husband and I
heard something come rushing towards us. It was
very dark but something rushed past me which
looked like a great animal, and went right over
the hedge. I distinctly saw a sort of big hound or
dog go over the hedge. I have absolutely no doubt
about it — namely, that it was a huge animal which
looked like a big hound which leaped over the
hedge. It certainly was not a horse or a donkey,
and it was not, of course, our own dog, who was
trembling at the back of us.
   Both my Husband and I were very frightened,
and the dog we had with us made an awful noise (a
frightened noise) and ran off back to Kington and
did not come back. [She also said their dog would
not afterwards come with them on this road.]
   Prior to that time, I had not heard of the
legend of the hound but my Husband then told me
about it, and said it undoubtedly was the hound.

                     Signed Emma Turner ?? 1919
```

I find my grandmother's statement most interesting. She stressed that the dog with them was a guard dog (probably used to patrol Arrow Lodge Mills at night), but on seeing the 'Hound' he turned and ran back to Kington as fast as he could. Dogs are very strange creatures; in the matter of the paranormal their senses are much more acute than those of a horse, whose defence is in flight. A horse will tell you all his life that a certain rock is actually a lion, and will shy each time he passes it!

My grandfather, Philip James Turner, dissuaded his young wife from saying anything about their experience on that horrible night, for fear that they would be thought 'moithered', or strange, which would certainly not do for a partner in the milling business with many clients! Another family story shows my grandfather's sturdy resistance to any 'weird' happening. Once when my father and grandfather were driving the pony trap back to Kington from New Radnor on a dark night in summer, they had just turned up from the Floodgates to the brow of the hill by the churchyard when the pony suddenly jibbed and would not go on. 'There's something frightening him in the churchyard,' said my grandfather, handing his son a lantern. 'Get down and see what it is.'

My father, who was only about ten at the time, was petrified, but he dared not disobey his father, so he scrambled up the wall and peered over. He saw a man asleep, and next to him a huge bear, also asleep. It was a 'travelling bear', sometimes known as 'dancing bears', which used to entertain market crowds – thankfully a thing of the past now, and against the law. My father scrambled down (very quietly!) and went back to the trap. Grandfather (who was a great horse man, and published a complete guide to horse care, including the care of draught horses) went to the pony's head and cajoled the frightened beast past with soothing words, whilst explaining to the boy what an extraordinary sense of smell a horse could have. Of course, this episode could have turned into yet another ghostly tale of Kington churchyard.

My father seems to have been more willing to listen to 'weird' tales then his father was; hence his interest in the statements he collected. He evidently sent copies of them to friends, for on 19 March 1919 Dorothy Banks wrote to him (see opposite). Mr. Bodenham, who was, I believe, a solicitor in Ludlow, had no connection with Kington except through his sister, and therefore no expectations of seeing anything amiss. One only hopes that the claret at dinner was not too generous!

Dear Mr. Turner

Many thanks indeed for so kindly sending me the
Nurse Fund subscription for the 4 years. I enclose
formal receipt. It is most interesting to hear of
your work in the Navy. Thank you also so much for
allowing us to see all these enclosures. It was a
pity, I think, that — while he was about it — Conan
Doyle should have chosen the name of an existing
old Herefordshire family & yet not the right one.
Traditions are varied and confusing enough in any
case! I looked last night in "Memorials of old
Herefordshire" & in the few numbers which came out
of the "Herefordshire Magazine" to see if I could
find anything more about the hound but I could not.
But Mrs Fidd Pratt told us the following story.
Miss Bodenham who lived at Belmont had a brother
staying with her years ago. They dined then at
about 5.30 pm & Mr. Bodenham was strolling in the
Churchyard after dinner, when to his astonishment
he saw a great black hound jump out of one of the
windows of the Vaughan Chapel. This was strange
enough, but what was his horror when, as he watched
it rush down between the tombstones & jump over
into the road, he saw the tombstones through it!
With regard to the Vaughan Arms of 3 heads with
snakes round their necks I see that one account
says that Thomas Ap Rosser (the "Black Vaughan")
who is himself in the Vaughan Chapel was born
with snakes growing out of the nape of his neck
& tied round it!! But a soberer account is that
one Vaughan — it does not say which — was left by
his nurse in the garden to finish his bread & milk
& when she returned a snake was coiled round the
child's neck & quietly feeding out of the same bowl
of milk! Again thanking you so much for your most
interesting enclosures herewith returned.

Believe me
Yours sincerely

Dorothy Banks

My father was also emboldened to write to Arthur Conan Doyle himself, thus:

Dear Sir,

I am a native of Kington, Herefordshire, and was recently spending a short holiday there.

I happened to hear that some little time ago, Mrs. Owens, the wife of the tenant of Hergest Court Farm, Nr. Kington (on which I believe your story, "The Hound of the Baskervilles" was based) 'had had a fright', but my informant did not tell me exactly what it was. Country people are usually a little reticent about such matters.

I have known Mr. & Mrs. Owens for many years, and I therefore had tea with them, and was shown over the old house which I believe dates back to the fourteenth century, and which is an extremely interesting old place.

Mrs. Owens very kindly furnished me with a Statement, of which I enclose copy, and which I think you would like to see.

I cannot, of course, criticise Mrs. Owens' statement — most probably what she heard was an old asthmatical rat. I can, however, say that she is an ordinary sensible woman of good education, and her husband farms a fairly large farm of about 350 to 400 acres.

Speaking as a Solicitor of 20 years experience, I should say she would make quite a good witness, and I should not fear her cross-examination by opposing Counsel.

After being in Kington, I went down to Worthing to see my Mother who is over 70, and was commencing to tell her about Mrs. Owens' experience, when she stopped me as she said she felt sure what I was about to say had to do with the Hound, and 'it brought it all back to her'. However, she allowed me to continue and then related to me her story of which I enclose copy.

I am, dear Sir,
Yours faithfully,

Cecil P. Turner

Conan Doyle's reply was brief and bland:

```
                                    Windlesham,
                                    Crowborough,
                                    Sussex

                                    Feb. 2nd

Dear Sir,

    My story was really based on nothing save a
remark of my friend Fletcher Robinson's that there
was a legend about a dog on the Moor connected with
some old family. I had no place in my eyes. What
you say is interesting and extraordinary.


                          Yours sincerely,

                          A. Conan Doyle
```

But as we have seen, that may not be the whole story ... This letter raises more questions than it answers. Did Conan Doyle really not know the legend of the Hound of the Vaughans, or did he have some reason for suggesting that he did not? If he did know the story, where had he heard it before? Is this another curious case of a dog that didn't bark? Whatever the truth, the mystery of the letter certainly raised the bidding at the auction!

Baskerville (above) and Hopton (below) crests

Appendix 2
A Note on the Baskervilles

Above the front door at Clyro Court is carved the family coat of arms. 'Argent' a chevron Jules between three 'heurts' (the latter are whimberries of deep purple colour that grow in the Welsh mountains). The crest is a wolf's head impaled on a spear, with five drops of blood. The motto is 'spero ut fidelis' – 'I hope as faithful' or 'hope through faith'. Undoubtedly this referred back to some brave ancestor several hundred years before. When the Baskervilles came over, there were many wolves in these parts. (The present names 'Bleddfa' and the 'Wolfpitts' at Walton are local references.)

The expression 'came over with the Conqueror' was often used by neo-Norman families, but in the case of the Baskervilles it seems to be well authenticated. Indeed, with the amount of royal blood reputed

Clyro Court

to have been in their veins, it is likely that they may have regarded William I as a bit of an upstart!

After 1066 they were granted lands based in Eardisley, called 'Herdledge' in the Domesday Book. It was here that they built a castle, and they built another near the Wye at Bredwardine. They do not appear to have been aggressively cruel in their administration, either towards the Anglo-saxons or towards the Welsh, who were their immediate neighbours. With the latter they made an important and politically astute alliance, through the marriage of Sir Robert Baskerville to Agnes, who was not only an heiress in her own right, but daughter of Nesta, who was herself the daughter of Rees ap Griffiths, Prince of south Wales. Their son also made a 'good' marriage, with Olwen of Eardisland, and their son, Sir Ralph Baskerville, married the daughter of Lord Clifford of nearby Clifford Castle, near Hay on Wye.

This connection brought about a well-known historical incident which ended in a duel and bloodshed. Sir Ralph Baskerville accused Lord Clifford of unjustly seizing Colwyn Castle, and challenged him to single combat in the churchyard at Llowes, where Lord Clifford was killed. Sir Ralph Baskerville obtained a pardon from the Pope, 'who was very angry that the church had been desecrated'. There is a strange upright stone in Llowes churchyard which tradition declares to mark the very spot where Lord Clifford met his end.

Although they probably played their part in the 'barons' wars', on the whole the family were far more interested in increasing their land-holdings, which they did to great effect over the years, owning huge estates in Wiltshire, Shropshire, Gloucestershire and as far as Sussex, as well of course as Herefordshire. They were powerful for five hundred years, but after the Civil War of 1645 they ceased to maintain Eardisley Castle, which was soon ransacked and burned down, finally becoming a farmhouse built largely out of the stones of the castle and still with the remains of a moat.

Meanwhile others of the Baskerville family had moved with the times and built themselves fortified manor houses, such as those at Pontrilas and Treago. By Arthur Conan Doyle's time the main family home was Clyro Court, built by Thomas Mynors Baskerville in 1839.

It is hardly surprising that in the years following the publication of Arthur's best-seller, Ralph Hopton Baskerville, who succeeded to Clyro

Court in 1904, was inundated with journalists, sightseers and other itinerant travellers, and nor is it surprising that he found it extremely intrusive. It was especially irksome that the Baskerville family had now become associated with the dreadful curse of the Black Hound, which had nothing to do with them at all.

My father was a member of that now almost extinct species, the family solicitor. He would never have divulged any of the secrets of his clients and was treated by them as a trusted friend. I believe he sent a letter on behalf of Ralph Baskerville to Arthur Conan Doyle, asking him for a definite assurance in writing – i.e. a disclaimer – that in spite of the title of *The Hound of the Baskervilles*, the Baskerville family of Clyro had nothing whatsoever to do with the Curse of the Vaughans. If my father received a reply it would be on private Baskerville family files, as he had written on their behalf. All he would say to us, his family, was that the reply had been unsatisfactory.

The only evidence we have that something definitely jolted Arthur is noted by Sir Christopher Frayling in a film he made about Arthur's life. As I have already mentioned, he points out that different editions of Arthur's acknowledgements in *The Hound of the Baskervilles* have different wording. In the first edition Arthur says that he owes 'the inception, the general plot and the local details' to Fletcher Robinson, but in the second edition he gives only a casual 'thank you' to Fletcher Robinson for 'a chance remark' that put him onto the story, and in referring to his written version of it makes a point of stating that 'every word is my own'.

There is only one surviving page of a manuscript to be found, and that, unsurprisingly, is in Arthur Conan Doyle's own handwriting. In his letters to his mother he inferred that he had written *half* the book before he had even reached Dartmoor. It is also interesting that when Fletcher Robinson gave a copy of the book to his coachman (who was called Baskerville and was sometimes thought to have provided Arthur with the name for the book), Arthur simply wrote a note, 'Thank you for letting the name be used' – not 'your name'.

Sometimes it seems that Arthur enjoyed the controversy and the publicity it created, and wished the truth to be left a mystery. There appears to be no written evidence that he had undertaken to make sure that the Baskervilles of Clyro were not implicated – and now there is no one living who knows otherwise.

Ralph Hopton Baskerville

On the back of the portrait photograph below, which belongs to my family, it says 'Ralph Hopton Baskerville b. Feb. 13th 1883. He succeeded to Clyro Court in 1904, when he came of age. The son of Walter Thomas Baskerville, who had married on Nov. 18th 1875 Bertha Maria (b. 1847 d. 1892) only surviving daughter and heiress of John Hopton, of Kemerton Court, Gloucestershire, and Canon Frome Court, Herefordshire, by Maria, daughter of Edward Dixon of Ashwood, Staffordshire.' Ralph was brought up partly at Canon Frome Court and partly at Clyro Court, which his grandfather had built in 1839. The 1891 Census shows that Ralph's two sisters, Sybil Maud and Dorothy Nesta were both of school age and living at Frome Court. Ralph was sent away to boarding school at Elmdale, Abbey Road, Great Malvern at the age of eight. Their mother seems to have divided her time between her own property at Kemerton Court, and Ralph's father, Walter, was often away managing more estates at Plympton St. Mary, Devon. The census shows eight servants at Frome Court, plus grooms, a governess and many gardeners.

When he was 18, Ralph joined the 1st Royal Dragoons. He would

have received a good training and, when the county was not on a war footing, plenty of leave. His passion was hunting. He was Master of the Radnor and West Hounds at Titley, and ran a pack in the Golden Valley and a private pack at Clyro and in Sussex. (What wonderful country it would have been to ride then – no barbed wire!) He was intensely interested in the breeding of his hounds, and for some of his packs would have incorporated the wiry coated Welsh hounds invaluable for hunting among rocks and in high places.

Above: Officers 2/1st Glamorgan Yeomanry, 1916
Back row: Vet Lt Laine, Lt G. Strick, 2nd Lt Lloyd, 2nd Lt Sabin Smith,
2nd Lt T.M. Bevan, Lt Hon C.N. Bruce, Lt Martin, 2nd Lt H.A. Christy,
2nd Lt Hearn, 2nd Lt Buckley, Lt V. Helme, 2nd Lt Shand
Centre: Capt Downes Powell, Major Morris, Major Hon O. Vivian, MVO, Lt Col C.
Venables Llewelyn, Major Marsham, Capt Baskerville, Capt H. Watson, Capt W. Lewis
Front: 2nd Lt H. Homfray, 2nd Lt Pearce, 2nd Lt Stockwood, 2nd Lt Pryce,
2nd Lt H.T. James with dog
Ralph Hopton Baskerville is 3rd from the right in the middle row

On the outbreak of war in 1914 Ralph was transferred to the
Glamorgan Yeomanry. They went to the Western Front in 1917 after
service in Egypt. (By that stage they were infantry.) Ralph was killed
on 18th April 1918. His grave is in Floegsteert Cemetery, Belgium, but
there is a memorial to him in Clyro churchyard:

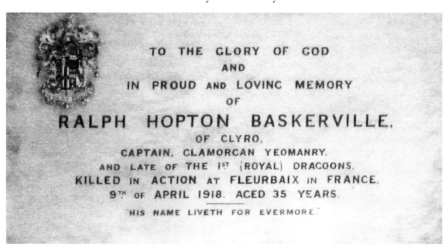

TO THE GLORY OF GOD
AND
IN PROUD AND LOVING MEMORY
OF
RALPH HOPTON BASKERVILLE,
OF CLYRO,
CAPTAIN, GLAMORGAN YEOMANRY,
AND LATE OF THE 1ˢᵀ (ROYAL) DRAGOONS,
KILLED IN ACTION AT FLEURBAIX IN FRANCE,
9ᵀᴴ OF APRIL 1918. AGED 35 YEARS.
"HIS NAME LIVETH FOR EVERMORE."

Clyro Court was later lived in by his sister Nesta, but the other side of the Baskerville family inherited it and finally sold it.

Hergest crest

Appendix 3
The Black Hound of Hergest and the BBC

My father continued to be keenly interested in the legend of the Hound. In 1931 he made the following note:

> In August 1931 we took a Bungalow on the top of Bradnor Hill, Kington for our holidays and the owner of the Bungalow kindly arranged for a woman named Mrs. Parker to come each morning to clean up for us. I remembered Mrs. Parker's parents quite well as I knew them when I was a boy.
>
> The first morning when I was there I said to Mrs. Parker in the presence of my wife 'you have curious things happen about here sometimes'. 'Ah yes' she replied, 'The Hound'. She went on to tell me how her husband saw it one evening as it was getting dusk and she told me also that there was no question her father died from the shock. She said that before he died her father told her mother that he had had a shock but would not say what it was. Mrs. Parker said she felt sure that her father shortly before his death had seen the Hound again. The Doctor himself said that her father had had a great shock.

Still on the scent of the Hound, in 1934 my father conducted the following correspondence with the BBC, on hearing that they were about to produce a place on the haunting of Hergest Court:

9th October, 1934

Dear Madam,
    I am a native of Kington, Herefordshire
and notice in my local paper that the legend
"The Black Dog of Hergest" has been dramatised
by you and will be broadcast from the Midlands
Regional Station on the 22nd instant.
    I have some statements in my possession
which I took down in reference to the Black
Dog and I think they will be of interest to
you. If you are in town and care to call at
this office I shall be very pleased to produce
them to you and perhaps you will telephone me
making an appointment.

                 Yours truly,
                   Cecil P. Turner

October 15 1934

Dear Sir,
    I have received your letter this morning,
and have despatched it immediately to the
Producer — Martyn Webster — at Midland
Regional Broadcasting House, Birmingham. I
cannot tell whether he will get in touch with
you or not. It is impossible for me to come
to London just now, although I am consumed
with curiosity and interest. At the earliest
possible moment I shall seek an interview.
 I think it is exceedingly kind of you to
write to me. I hope you will be able to listen
to the play on Oct. 22, and any comments you
chose to send afterwards to the Producer
would, I know be greatly appreciated.
    I am a native of Leominster — I wonder if
you recognise the name?

                 Again thanking you,
                 Believe me,
                 Very sincerely,
                 Helen M. Enoch

October 15th, 1934

Dear Miss Enoch,

Many thanks for your letter and enclosure. I think it would be much better, as Mr. Turner wrote to you and not to the B.B.C., if you would write and ask for the papers in question to be sent to you (or copies if they are of value). It looks as though there might be something of real interest.

I'm so glad you will be able to be with us on Wednesday, October 17th.

I return letter herewith.

Yours sincerely,

Martin C. Webster

Oct. 16 1934

Dear Mr. Turner,

I enclose letter received last night from the producer of 'The Black Dog'. Is it possible for me to see the papers without coming to London? I fear not! I think probably you are in possession of some knowledge, unknown to me, the inclusion of which would materially strengthen the play. We begin rehearsals tomorrow (Wednesday evening).

I am very grateful for your kind interest in the matter. I wish I could get up to town now — but it is quite impossible at the moment.

I am
Yours very faithfully

Helen M. Enoch

16th October, 1934

Dear Madam,

I am much obliged by your letter of
yesterday's date. I am sorry I was out when you
telephoned.

I enclose the statements which I referred
to in my previous letter, but on the distinct
understanding that they are only made use of for
your broadcast and that neither my mother's name
nor Mrs. Owens's is mentioned. I particularly do
not desire that these statements shall appear in
any newspapers and if I can do so I reserve the
copyright in them. My whole object is of course to
avoid any publicity in the matter.

I may say that as boys we were always very
nervous about the Hergest Court Road. I was at the
Grammar School, Kington with two of the Vaughans.

Yours sincerely,

Cecil P.Turner

P.S. Both my mother and Mrs. Owens were extremely
sensible women.
P.P.S. Please return the enclosed when finished
with.

(It is thought the Hound only comes out now to
foretell the death of a Vaughan.)

Oct. 18 1934

Dear Sir,
     I found the registered envelope awaiting
me late last night. A thousand thanks! Your
wishes shall be respected in every detail. I
am most thrilled, because I have written the
first scene in Hergest Court 100 years ago
— a conversation between the caretaker and a
friend — and they hear the whining & snuffling
of a hound in the house, although their own
dog is outside. I had no idea that real
events were so near my imaginative efforts.
The Producer is most anxious to see these
papers. I think it most awfully good of you
to trust them to me. I will see that they are
returned to you intact by registered post.
I had the pleasure of knowing the late Sir
Arthur Conan Doyle — through literary work. My
mother (aged 83) is tremendously interested in
your communication. She was born quite near
Hergest, and has lived round about Kington and
Leominster all her life until the last two
years with me here in Birmingham. My father
was a J.P. for Leominster.
     Again thanking you,
     Believe me
          Very sincerely yours
               Helen M. Enoch

Oct. 18 1934

Dear Sir,

Collie Knox is coming to rehearsal this evening; in deference to your wishes re publicity, I am returning these papers, to be quite sure he does not purloin them for the Daily Mail. The B.B.C. and I send our thanks and appreciation of your interest.

Yours very sincerely
Helen M. Enoch

20th October, 1934

Dear Miss Enoch,

I am much obliged by your letter of yesterday's date returning the papers which I sent you.

I have a dread of the present-day journalist as he seems to make everything the subject of ridicule.

I hope your broadcast will be a great success.

With kind regards,
Yours very sincerely,
Cecil P. Turner

Appendix 4
The importance of Hergest Court

When the serfs of the 12th century were busy building the massive structure of Hergest Court they may have had some idea of its strategic importance. The design was ambitious, using the River Arrow partly as a moat facing the early Castle Twts on its 'tump'. (A tump is the local name for a mound, and this was quite probably a tumulus.) Hergest Court controlled the valley leading to the church and the old settlement of Kington, which in turn was protected by a secondary (probably timber) castle facing Bradnor Hill. They certainly would not have known, however, what an extraordinary part of Great Britain this was, and what importance it would come to have, historically, geographically and archaeologically.

Only recently, in 1996, an enormous wood henge, now dated to 2,500 BC, was spotted from the air in the Radnor Valley. Covering 75 acres, this egg-shaped henge has a central *ffynnonau* or spring and was built of oak. It is believed to pre-date Avebury and Stonehenge by a thousand years. Later, in the Bronze Age, the 'Four Stones' were placed nearby – mysterious standing stones of the rare 'green' stone brought across from Stanner. Another of these 'green' stones is now in Radnor Church, reshaped by the Christians as a font.

These Celts left behind some beautiful gold work. Near the hill known as 'the Smatcher' in the Radnor Valley were found two exquisite bracelets now in the National Museum of Wales.

Then came the Romans, who established their 'marching camps' up and down the border. They left a hoard of silver, discovered during the First World War (and now also in the Welsh Museum at Cardiff), at Corton, Presteigne, near what was their Holy Spring.

Later the Welsh fought the Mercians, whose King Offa built the famous Dyke which runs from at least Bradnor Hill northwards; there is continuing debate about what line it might have taken to the south, or if indeed its course ever ran further south. And next came the Normans, whose finely made castles sprang up everywhere, their legacy probably making the landscape one of the most picturesque in the whole of the country. Gradually, however, castles became obsolete and fortified manor houses took their place, their great beauty again enhancing the natural scene.

Then it was the time of the geologists. In Georgian and Victorian times the uniqueness of this area was realised, and brought the great Sir Roderick Murchison to these parts. For several years he stayed in Presteigne with his wife Charlotte (née Hugonin), herself a talented artist. She was friendly with Joseph Murray Ince, the artist, who lithographed *The Seven Views of Radnorshire*. As Charlotte was French-born, she enjoyed conversing with Anne-Elizabeth Ince, Joseph's mother, who was also French.

The part of Hergest Court visible from the road today faces north and has an Elizabethan aura. This is because it was inherited at that time by Margaret Vaughan, who married Sir John Hawkins of sea-going fame. He had been married twice before and when he wedded Margaret Vaughan she was past child-bearing age. However, I am (although no genealogist) of the opinion that her stepsons may have asked her for a few of her wide acres. There are at least two very successful farming Hawkins families in the district now who may have owed their start to the generous Lady Hawkins, who also founded the famous Lady Hawkins Grammar School in Kington. At Hergest she employed the famous worker in wood John Abel, whose carvings are to be seen in many Herefordshire churches.

How sad it is that the Hergest Court we read about in history, with its 'eight towers', its refectories and its library, which housed the 'Red Book of Hergest', a unique chronology of events and Bardic poems, has gone. The Red Book itself is safely in the Bodleian Library in Oxford; it is even older than the 'Black Book of Carmarthen', which is in the National Library of Wales in Aberystwyth.

When Tomas Vaughan, the son of Roger Vaughan of Bredwardine, inherited Hergest Court and married Ellen Gethin in around 1440, what a wonderful place Hergest must have been! And how foolish of that hot-headed young man to swear an oath to the Devil which brought a curse on his family for several hundred years!

Index